Wolfgang Amadeus Mozart

LATER SYMPHONIES

Full Orchestral Score
of Symphonies 35-41
from the Breitkopf & Härtel
Complete Works Edition

DOVER PUBLICATIONS, INC., NEW YORK

Contents

NOTE: In Symphony No. 37, only the *Adagio maestoso* introduction is by Mozart; the remainder is by Michael Haydn.

Published in Canada by General Publishing Company, Ltd.,
30 Lesmill Road, Don Mills, Toronto, Ontario.
Published in the United Kingdom by Constable and Company, Ltd.,
10 Orange Street, London WC 2.

This Dover edition, first published in 1974, is an unabridged republication of Volume III *(Dritter Band)* of Series 8 *(Serie 8. Symphonien)* of *Wolfgang Amadeus Mozart's Werke. Kritisch durchgesehene Gesammtausgabe*, originally published by Breitkopf & Härtel, Leipzig, in 1880-1882. English titles have been substituted for the German designations in the Breitkopf & Härtel edition.

International Standard Book Number: 0-486-23052-X
Library of Congress Catalog Card Number: 74-75929

Manufactured in the United States of America
Dover Publications, Inc.
180 Varick Street
New York, N. Y. 10014

SYMPHONY No. 35
in D Major, K.385 ("Haffner")

Composed July 1782 in Vienna.

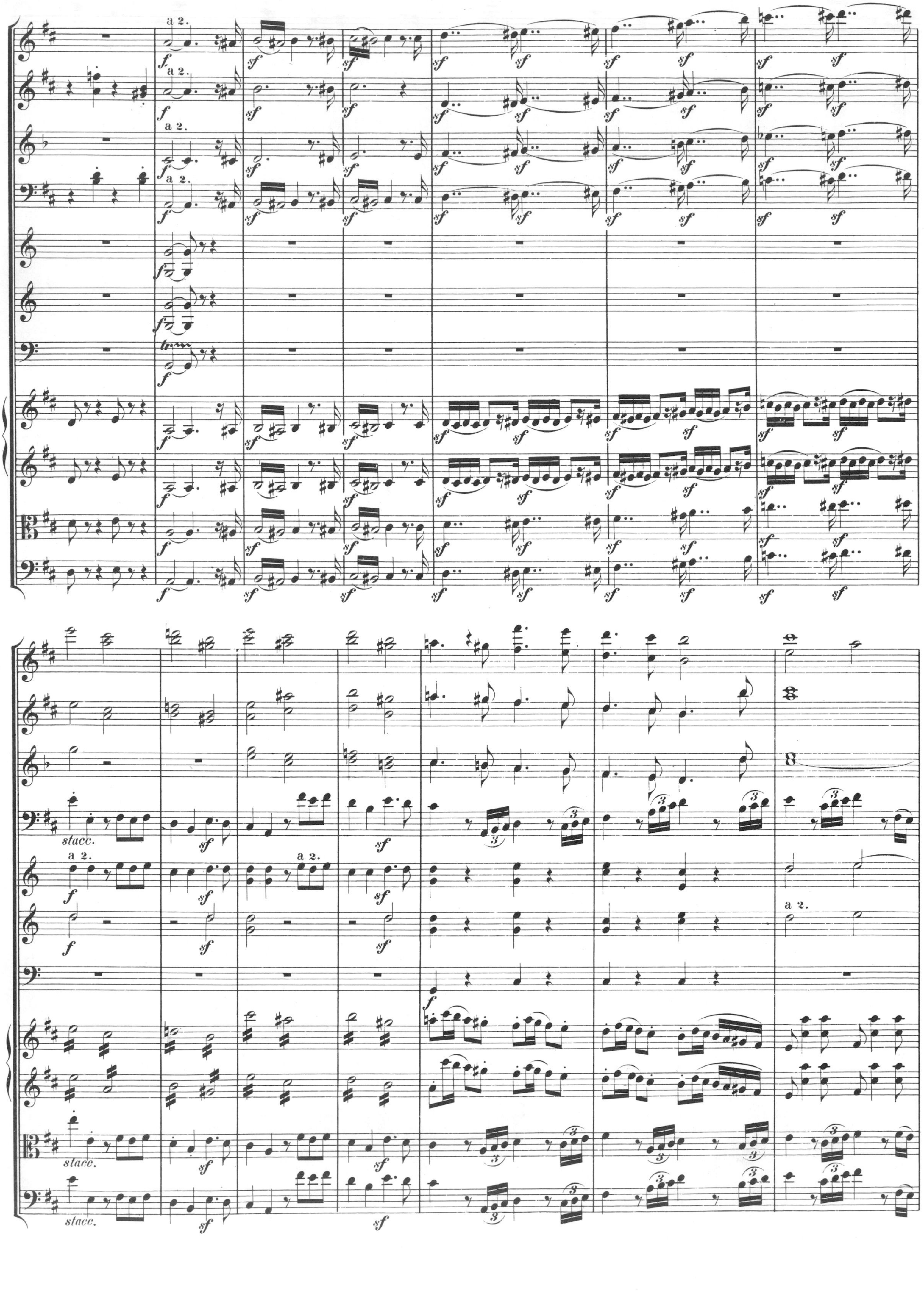
a 2.
f
sf
stacc.

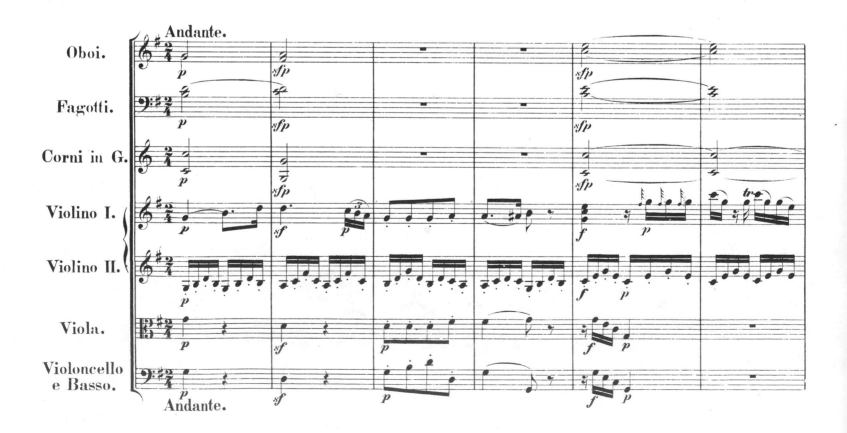

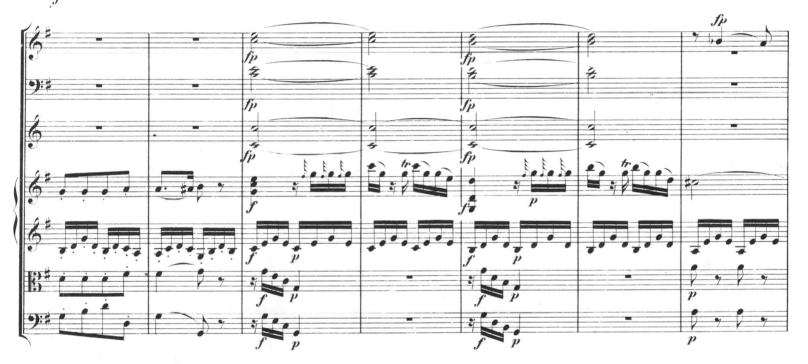

MENUETTO.

Trio.

Menuetto da Capo.

FINALE.
Presto.

Flauti

Oboi.

Clarinetti in A.

Fagotti.

Corni in D.

Trombe in D.

Timpani in D.A.

Violino I.

Violino II.

Viola.

Violoncello
e Basso.

Presto.

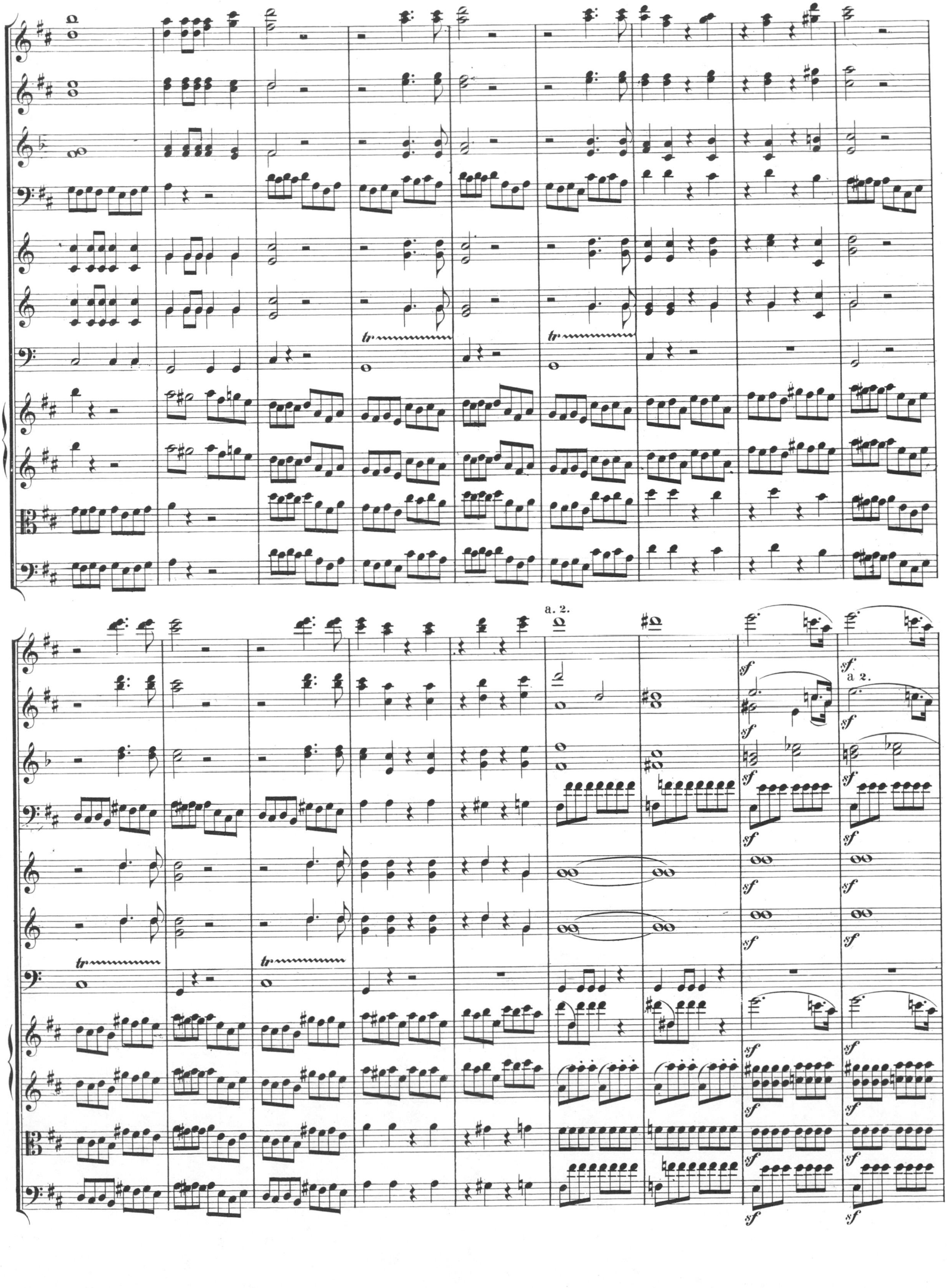
a. 2.
a 2.

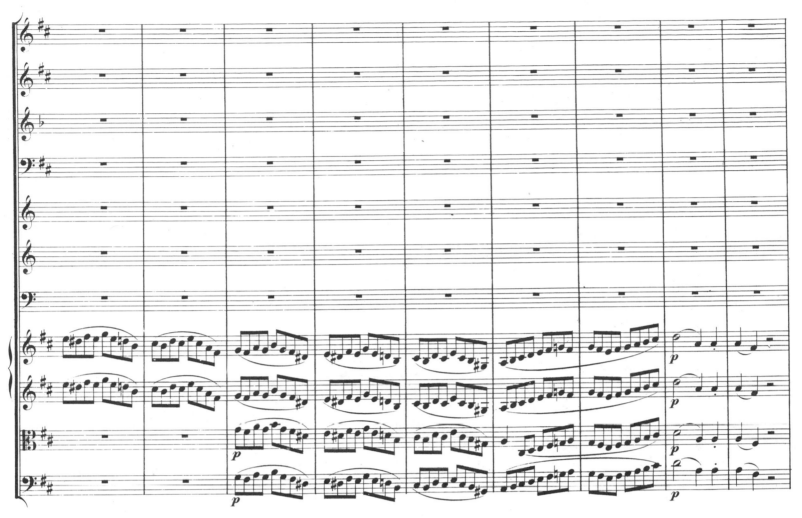

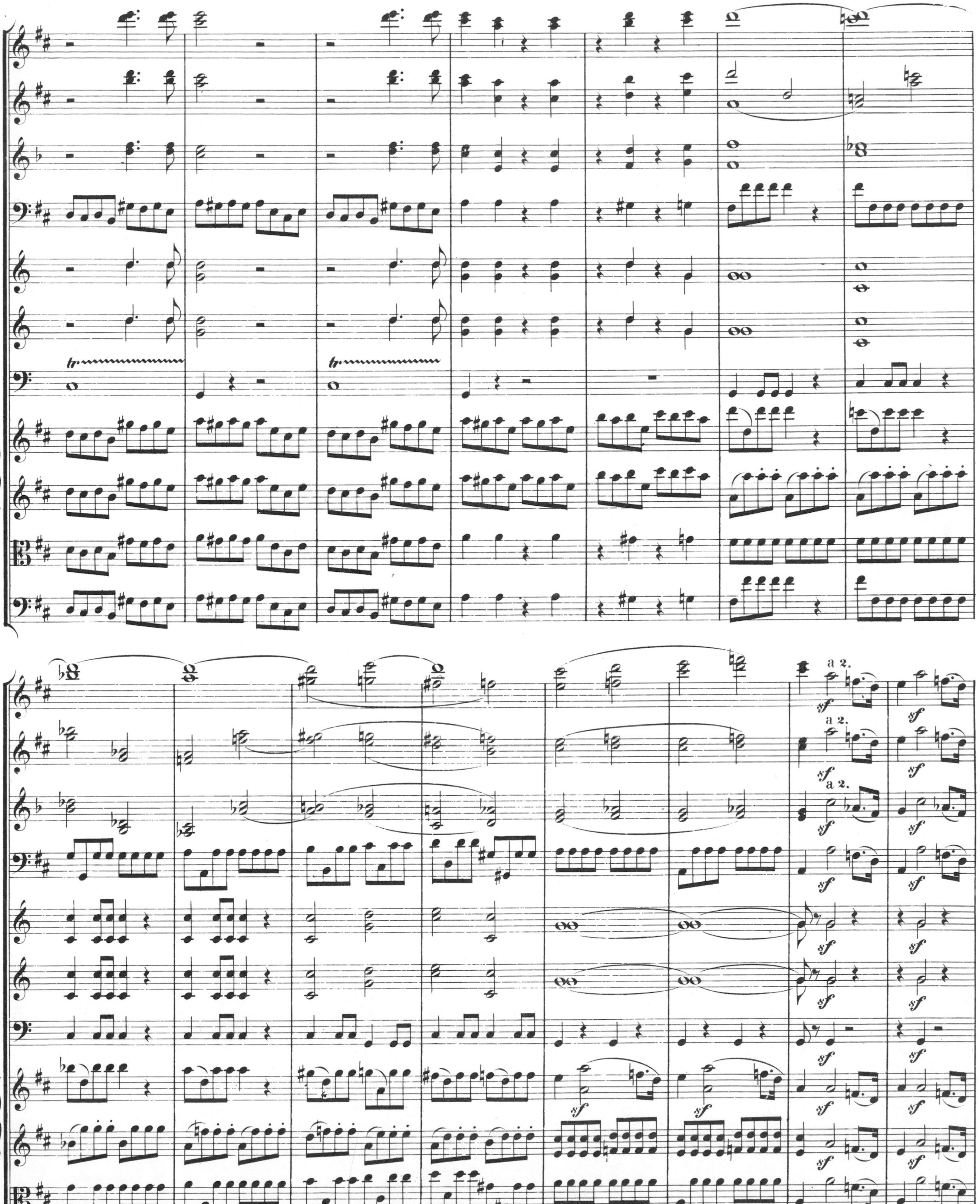
tr
tr
a 2.
a 2.
a 2.
sf

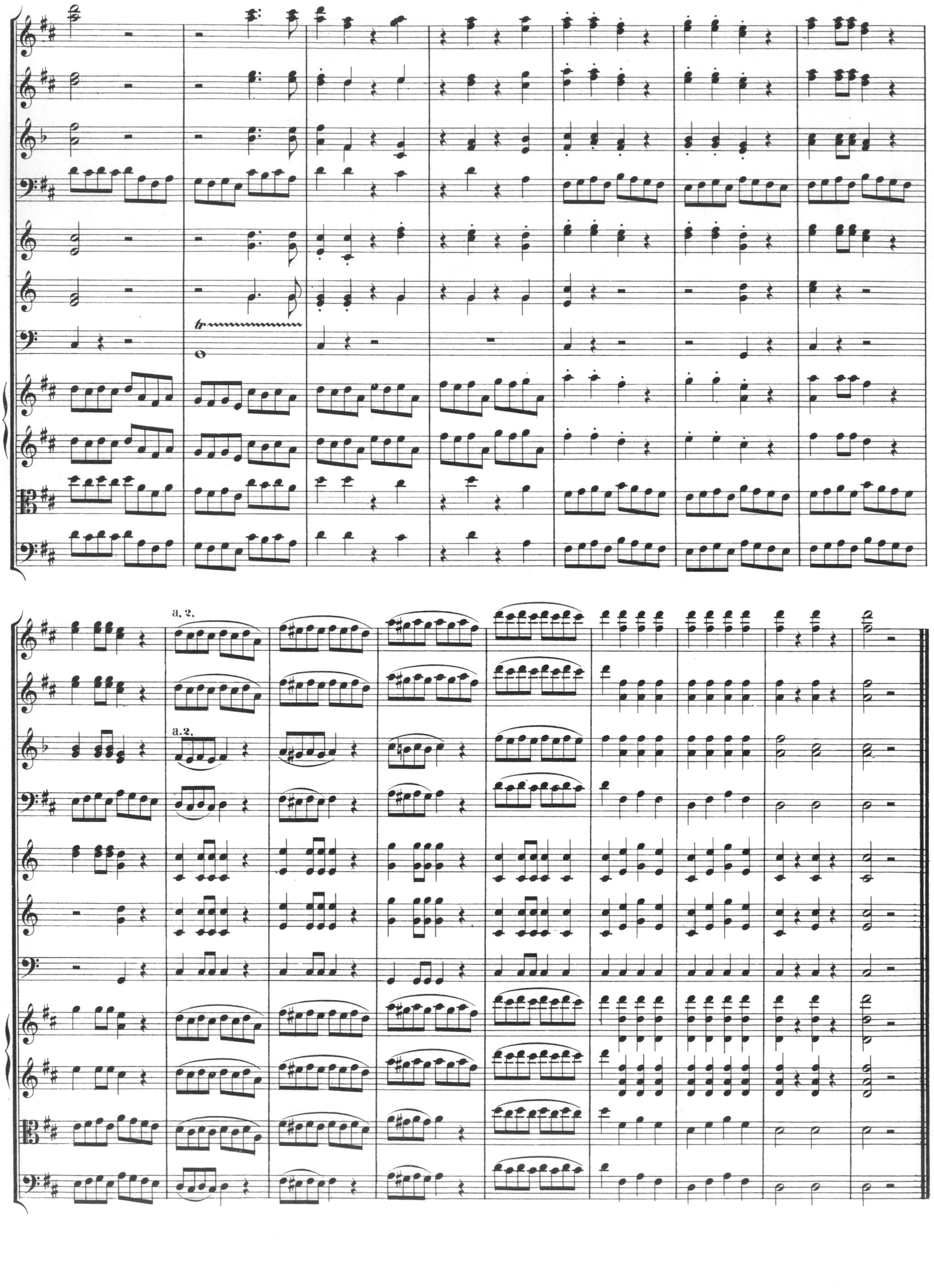
tr
a. 2.
a.2.

SYMPHONY No. 36
in C Major, K.425 ("Linz")

Composed November 1783 in Linz.

Allegro spiritoso.

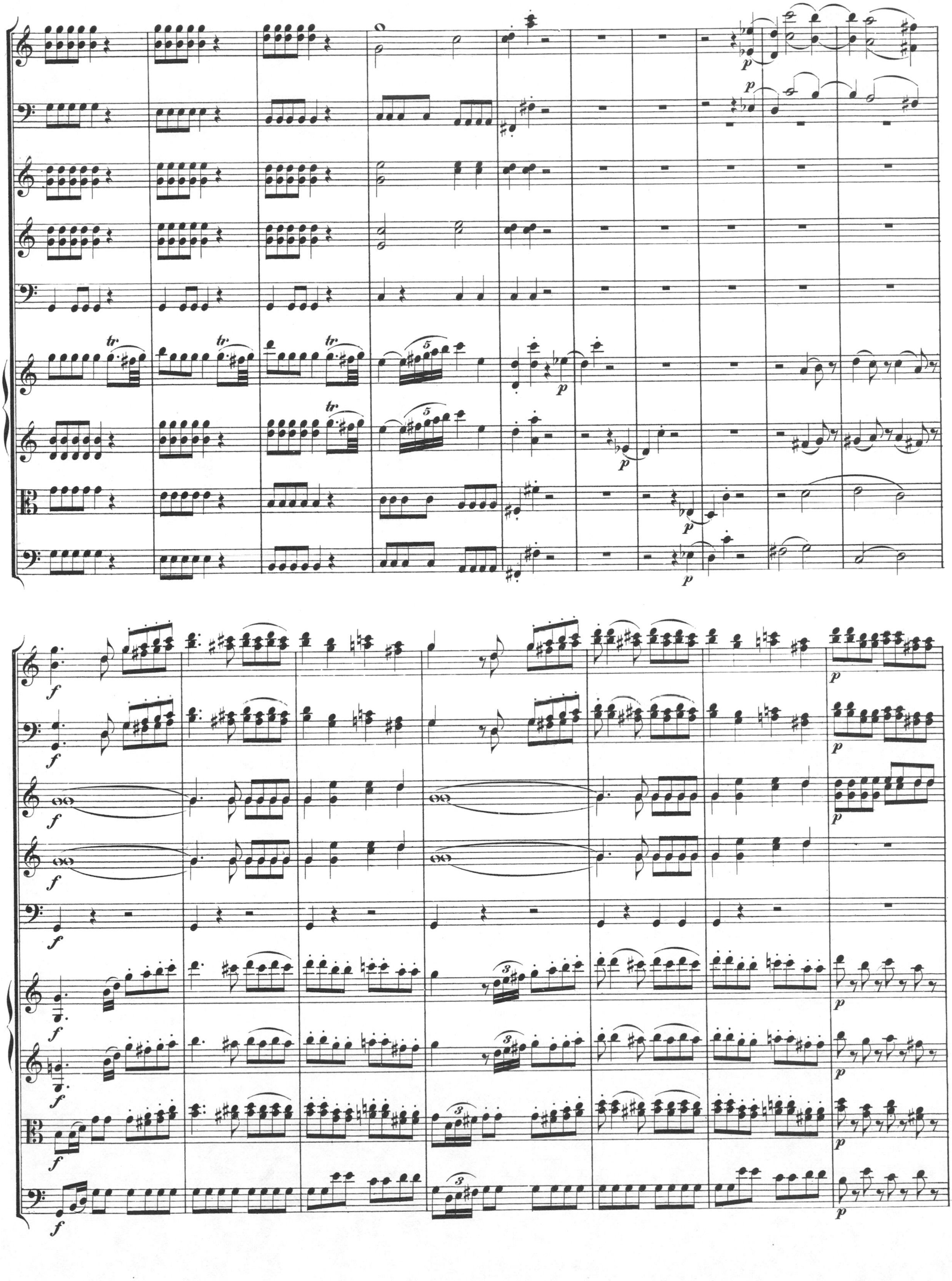
tr
5
3
p
f

Poco Adagio.

Oboi.

Fagotti.

Corni in F.

Trombe in C.

Timpani in C.G.

Violino I.

Violino II.

Viola.

Violoncello e Basso.

MENUETTO.

Oboi.

Fagotti.

Corni in C.

Trombe in C.

Timpani in C. G.

Violino I.

Violino II.

Viola.

Violoncello e
Basso.

Trio.

Menuetto da Capo.

SYMPHONY No. 37
in G Major, K.444
Said to be composed in 1783.

Allegro con spirito.

Andante sostenuto.

Flauto.

Corni in C.

Violino I.

Violino II.

Viola.

Violoncello
e Basso.

Oboi.

Corni in G.

Violino I.

Violino II.

Viola.

Violoncello
e Basso.

Allegro molto.

SYMPHONY No. 38
in D Major, K.504 ("Prague")

Composed December 1786 in Prague.

Allegro.

Allegro.

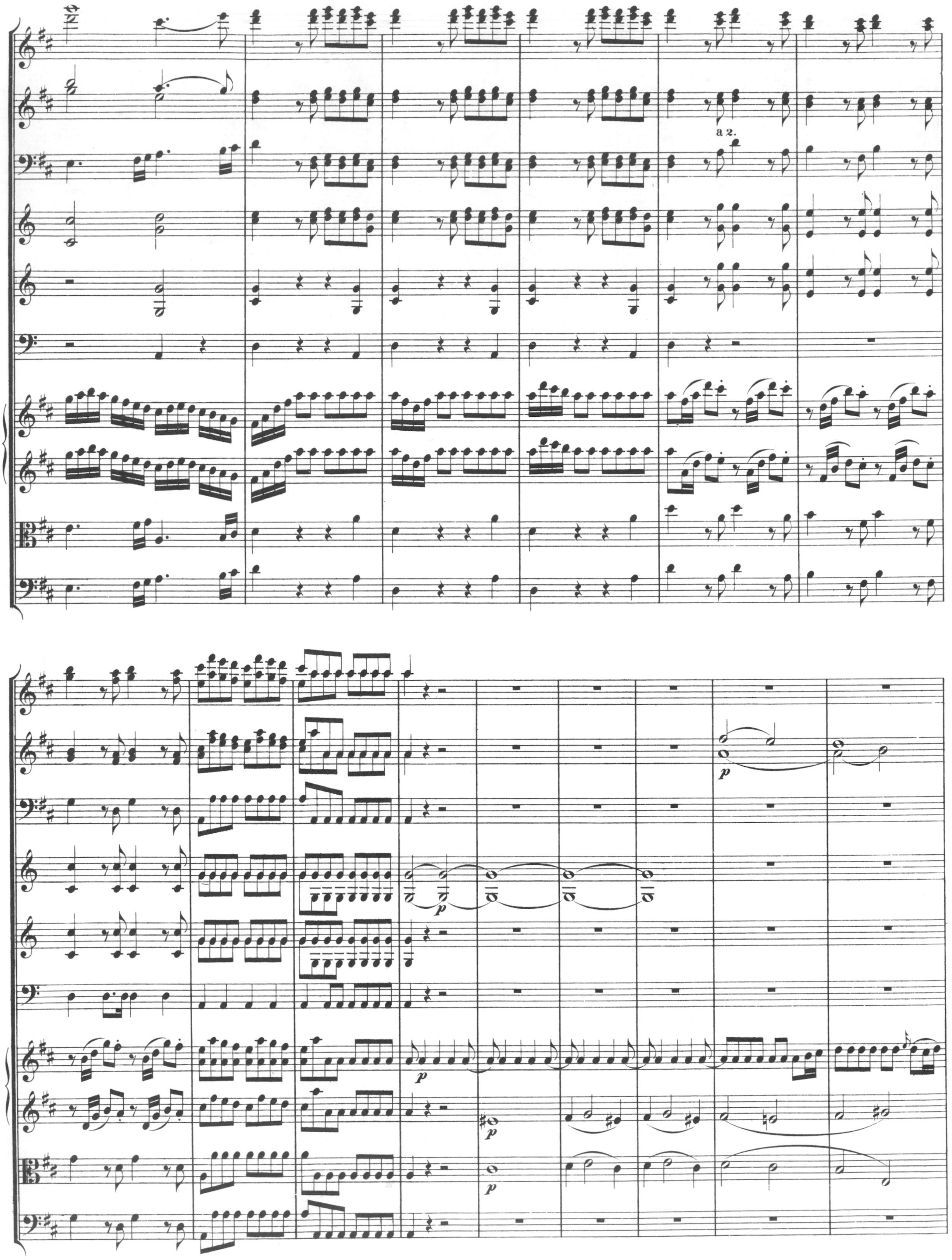
a 2.
p

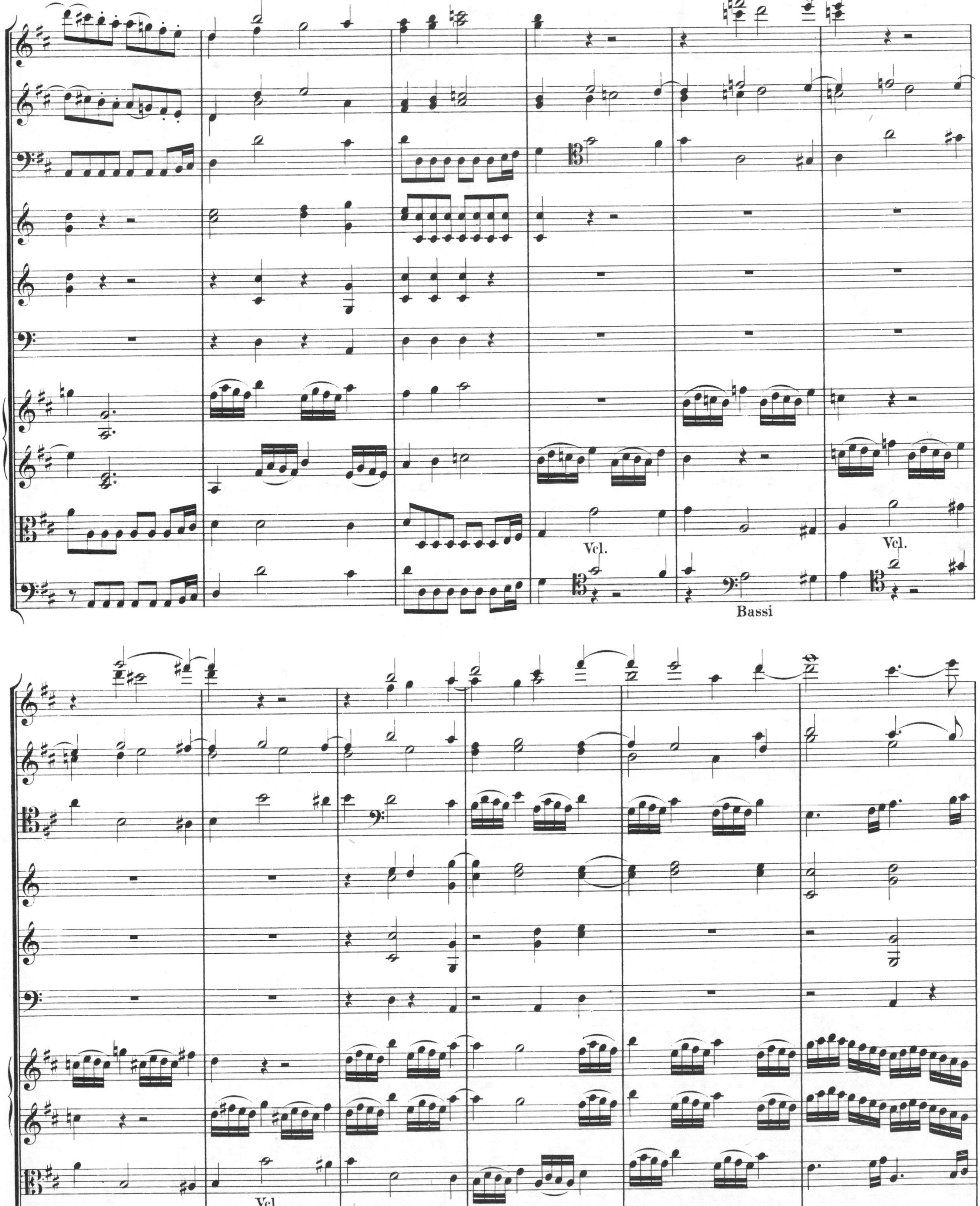
Vcl.
Bassi
Vcl.
Bassi
Vcl.
Bassi

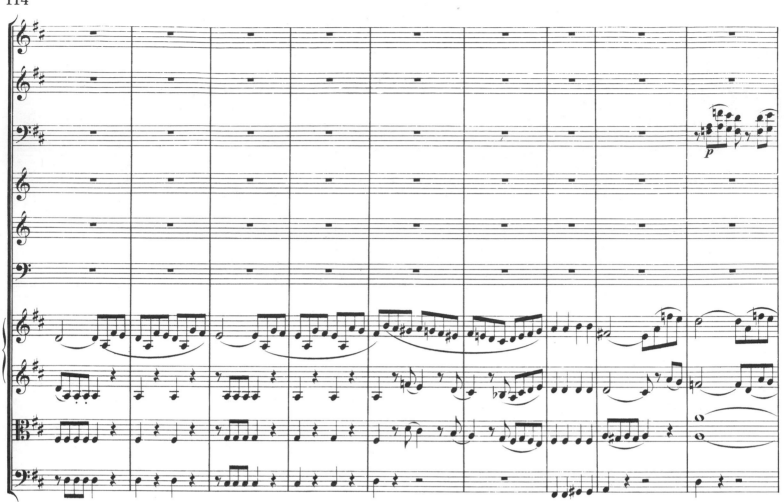

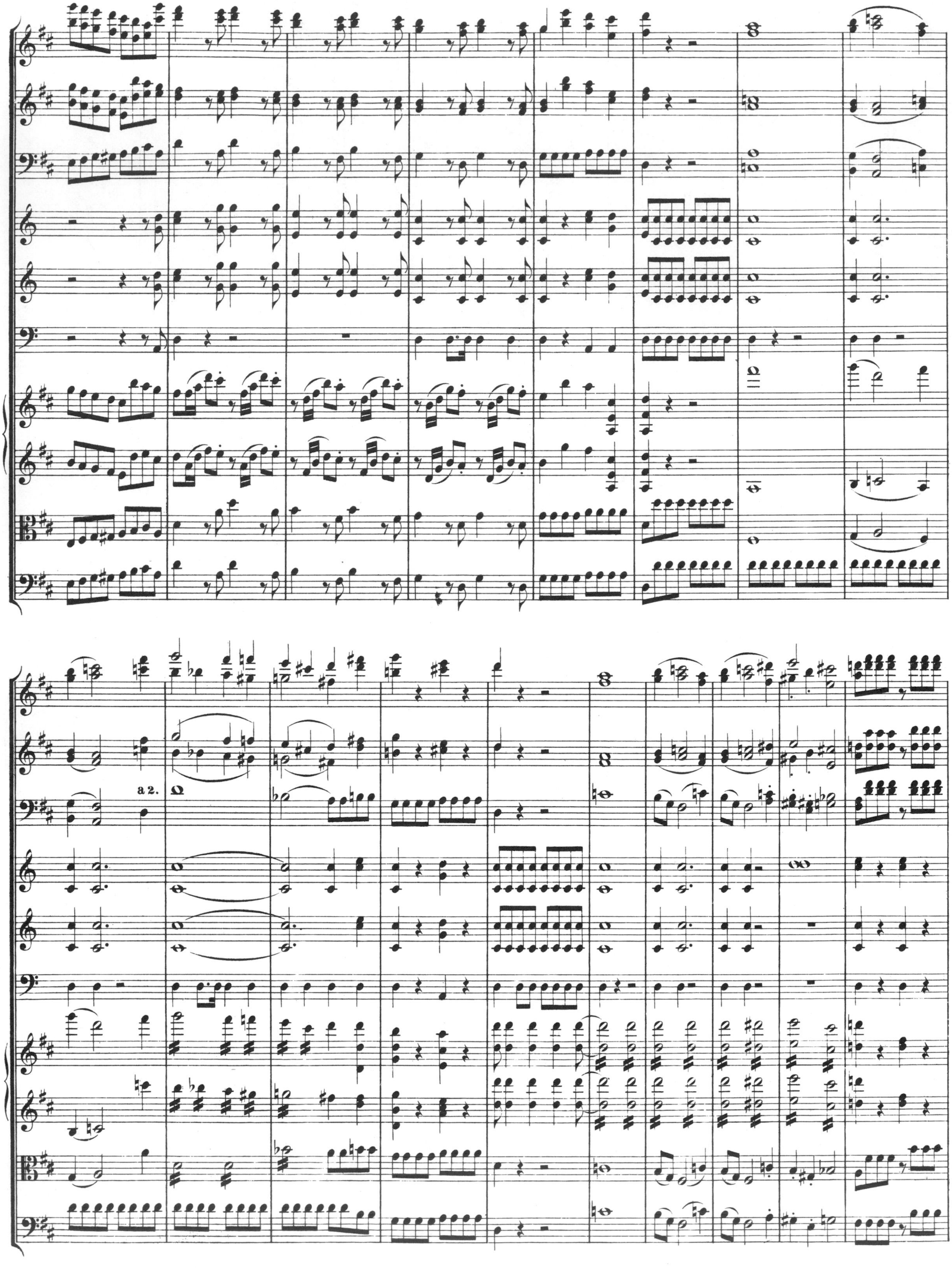
a 2.

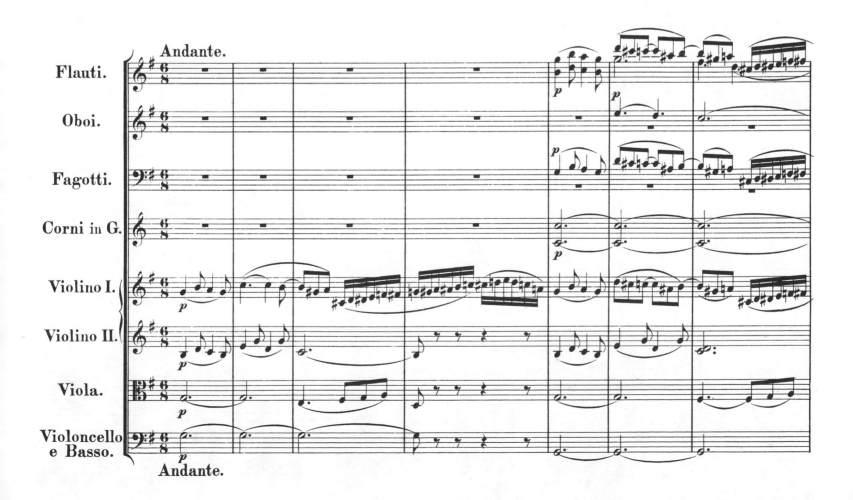

Flauti.

Oboi.

Fagotti.

Corni in G.

Violino I.

Violino II.

Viola.

Violoncello
e Basso.

Andante.

Andante.

FINALE.
Presto.

Flauti.

Oboi.

Fagotti.

Corni in D.

Trombe in D.

Timpani in D.A.

Violino I.

Violino II.

Viola.

Violoncello e Basso.

Presto.

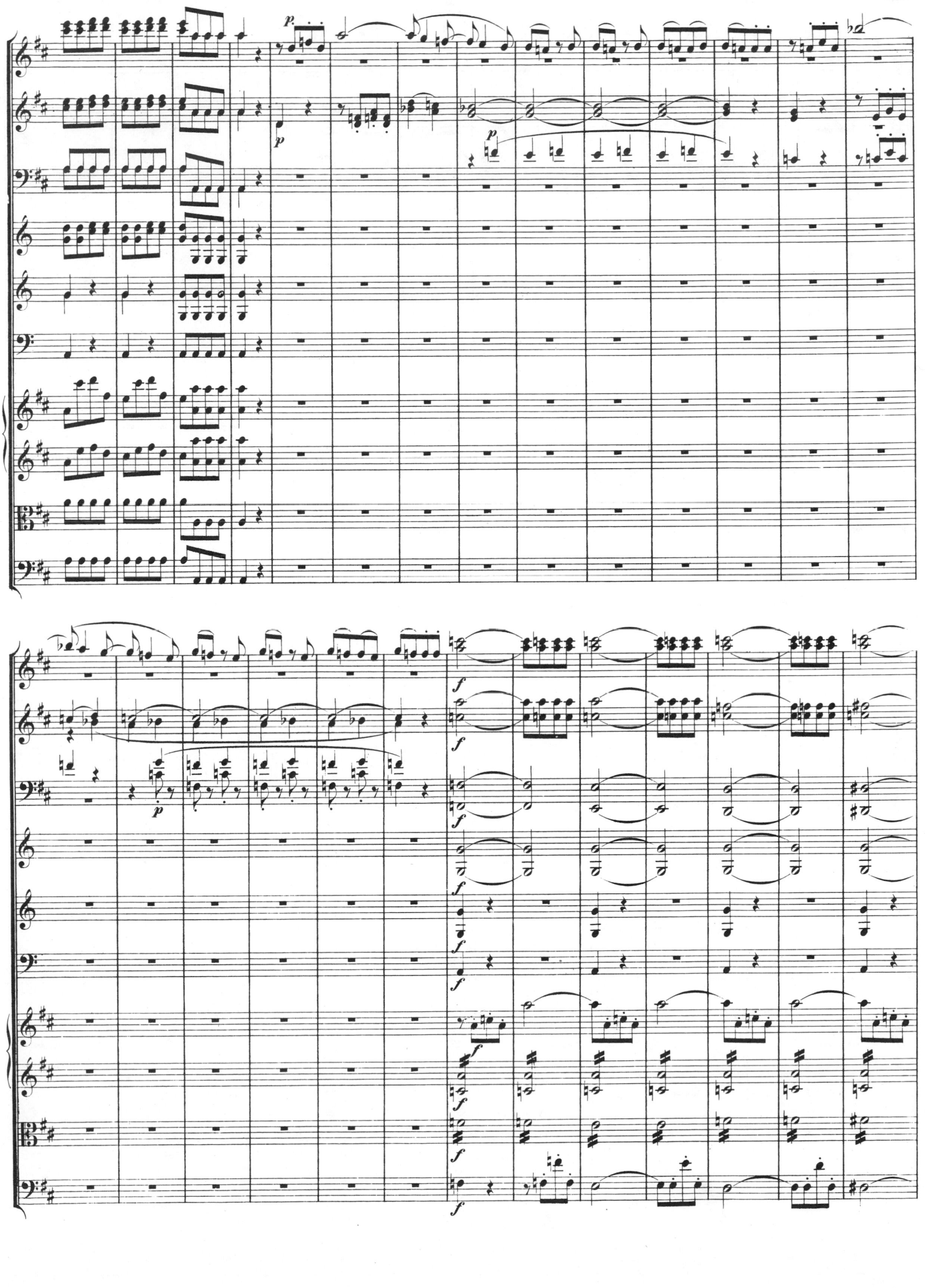

SYMPHONY No. 39
in E-flat Major, K.543
Composed June 1788 in Vienna.

Allegro.

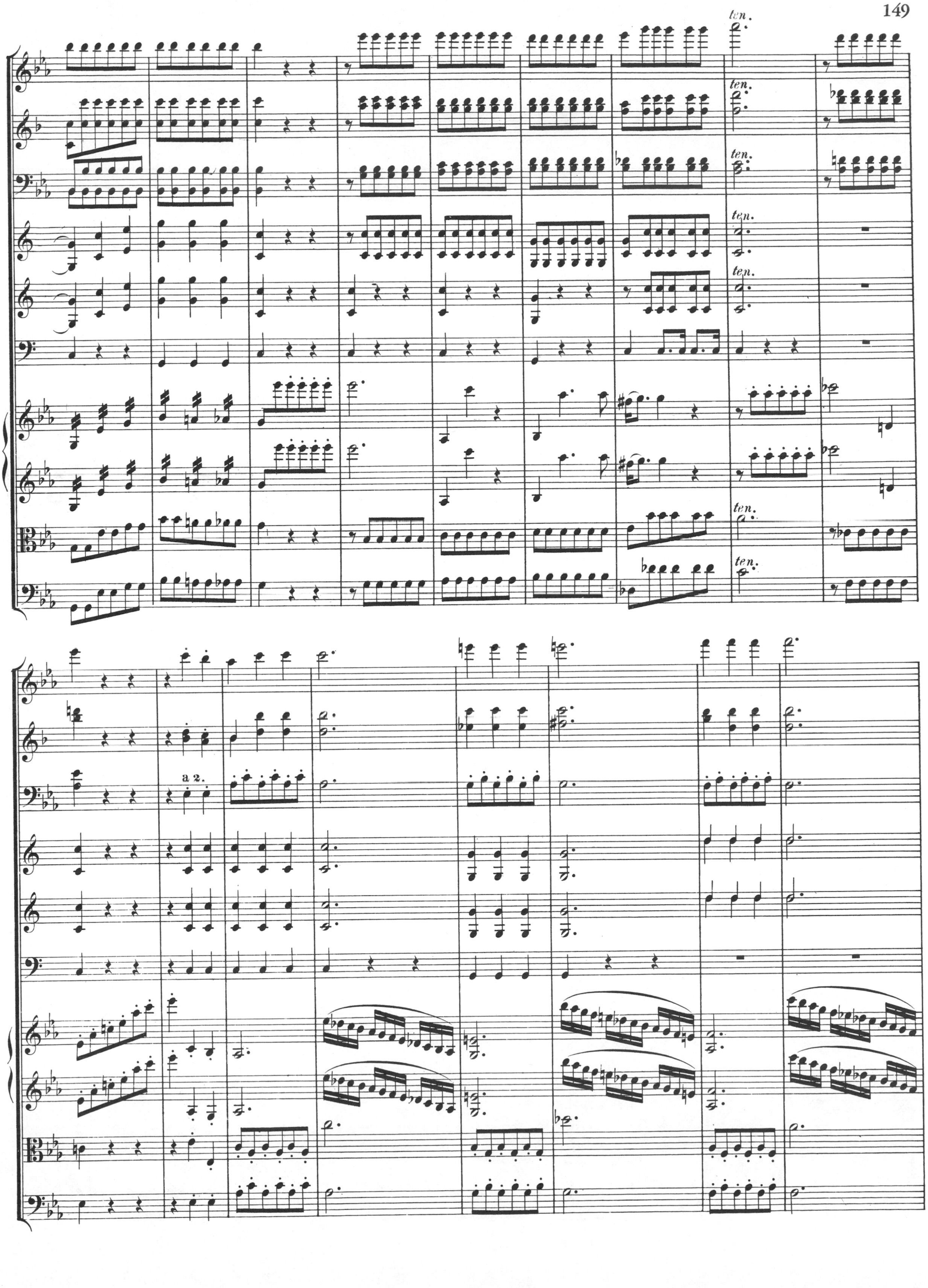
ten.
ten.
ten.
ten.
ten.
ten.
ten.
a 2.

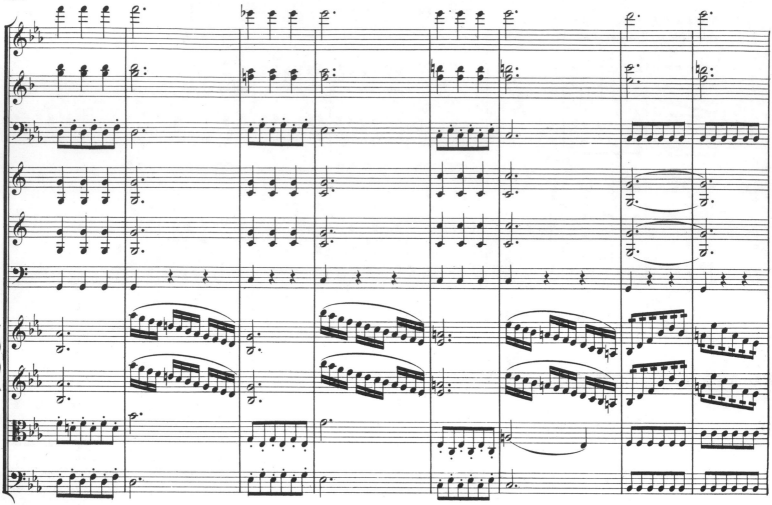

154

			Andante con moto.
Flauti.		
Clarinetti in B.		
Fagotti.		
Corni in Es.		
Violino I.		
Violino II.		
Viola.		
Violoncello e Basso.		

MENUETTO.
Allegro.

Trio.

Men. D.C.

Finale.
Allegro.

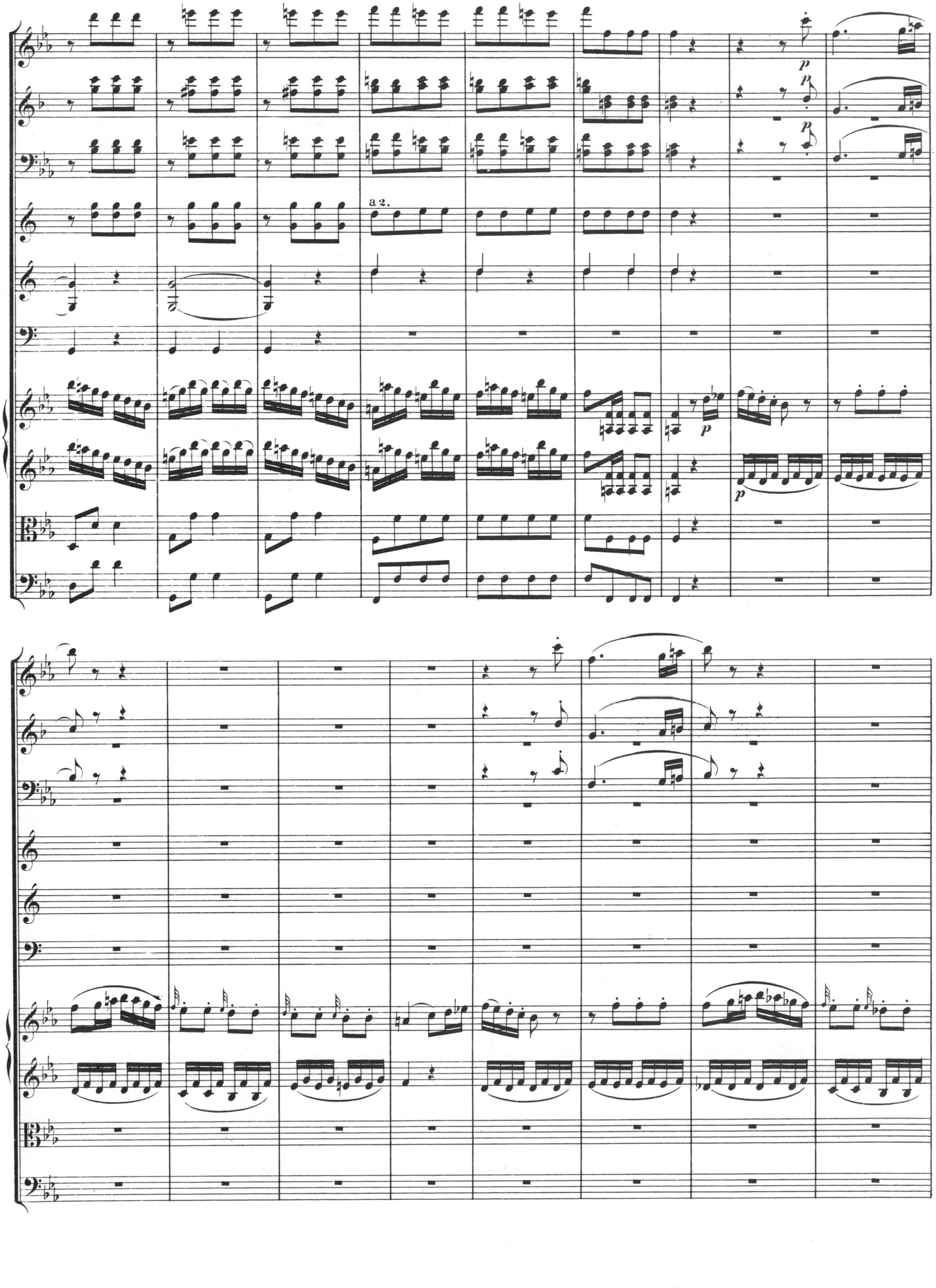
a 2.

SYMPHONY No. 40
in G Minor, K.550

Completed July 25, 1788 in Vienna.

The Oboe and Clarinet parts printed in the two systems at the top were added later by Mozart to replace the Oboe part in the fourth system.

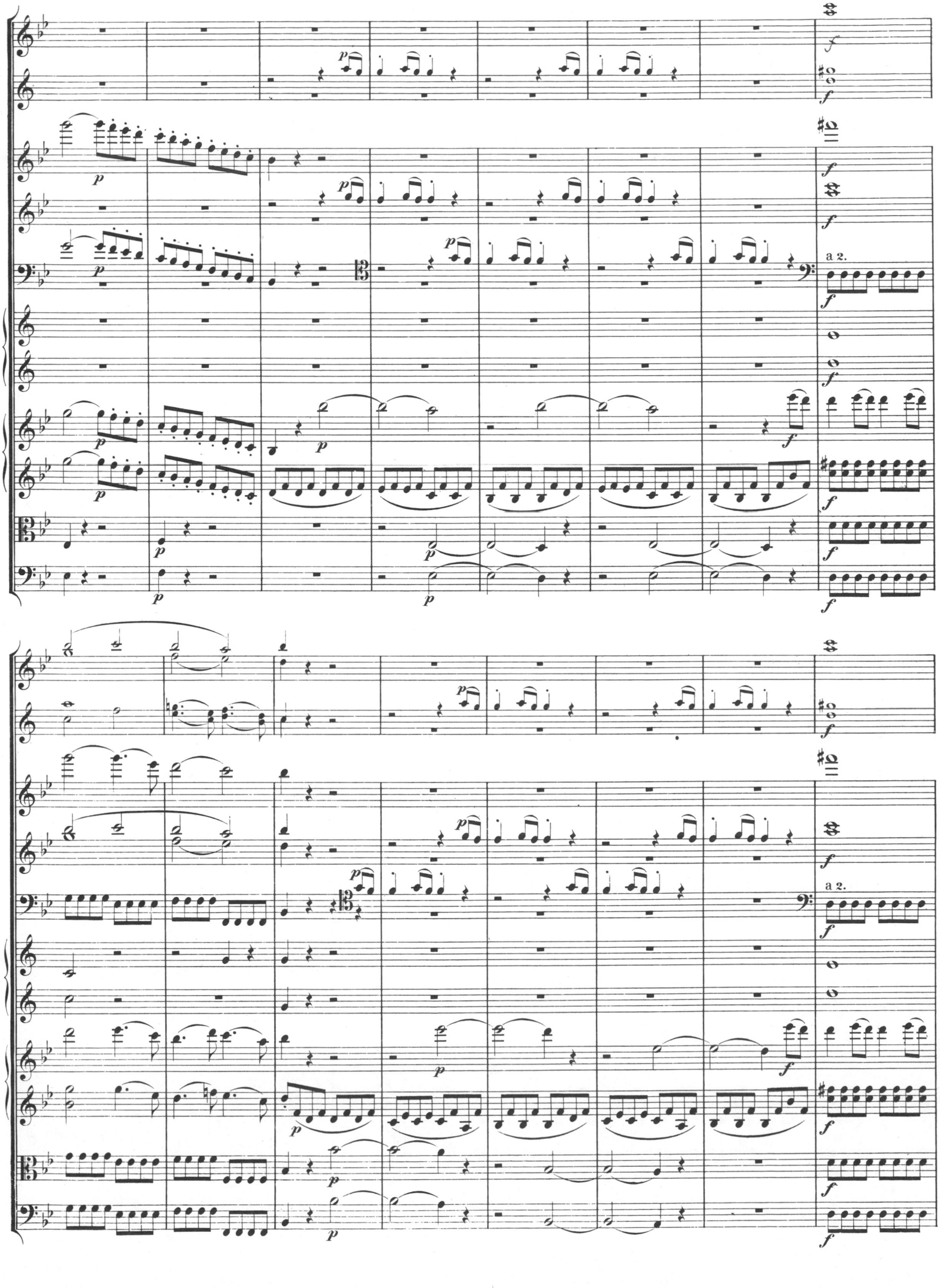
a 2.
a 2.

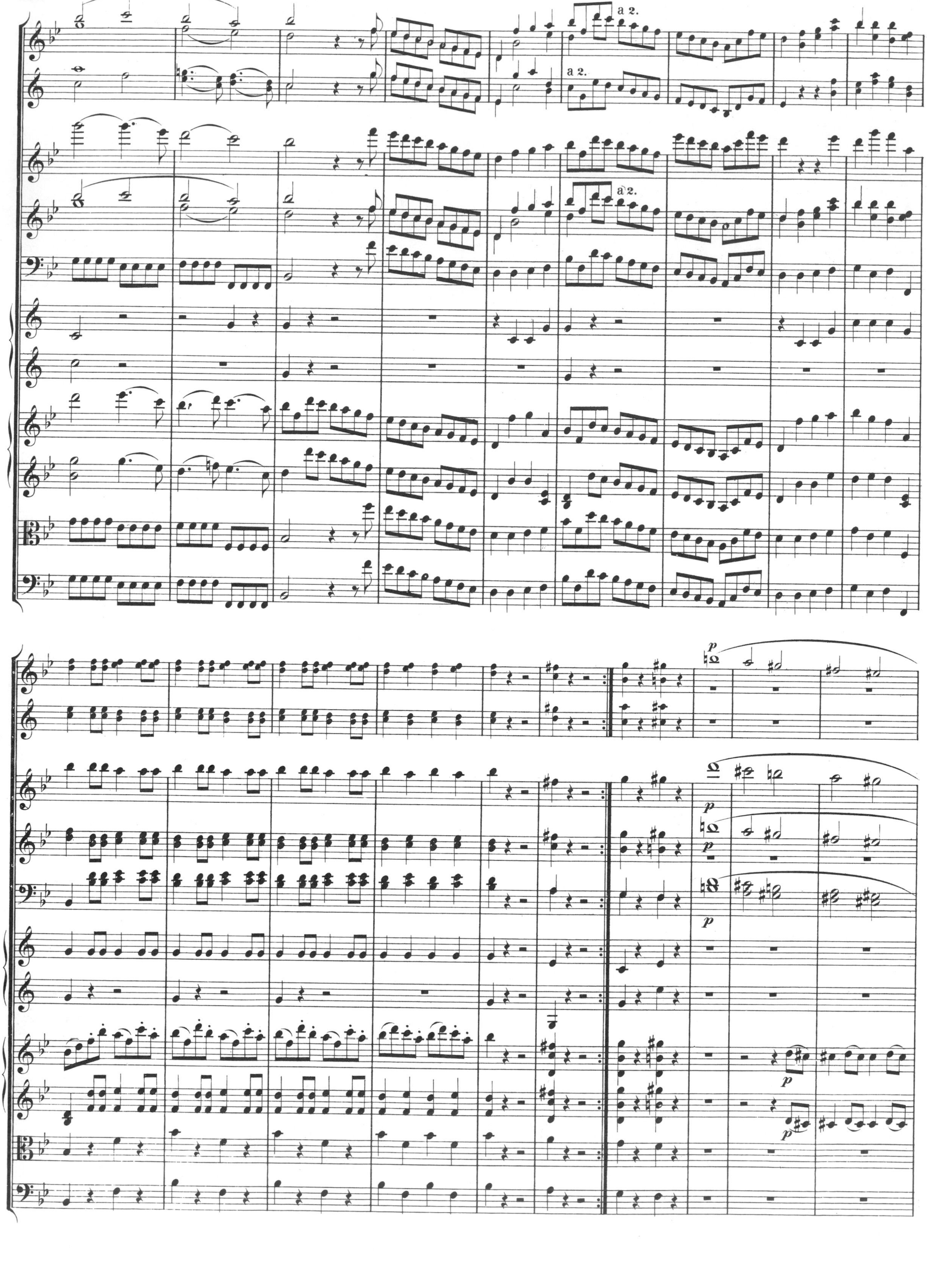
a 2.
a 2.
a 2.
p
p
p
p
p
p

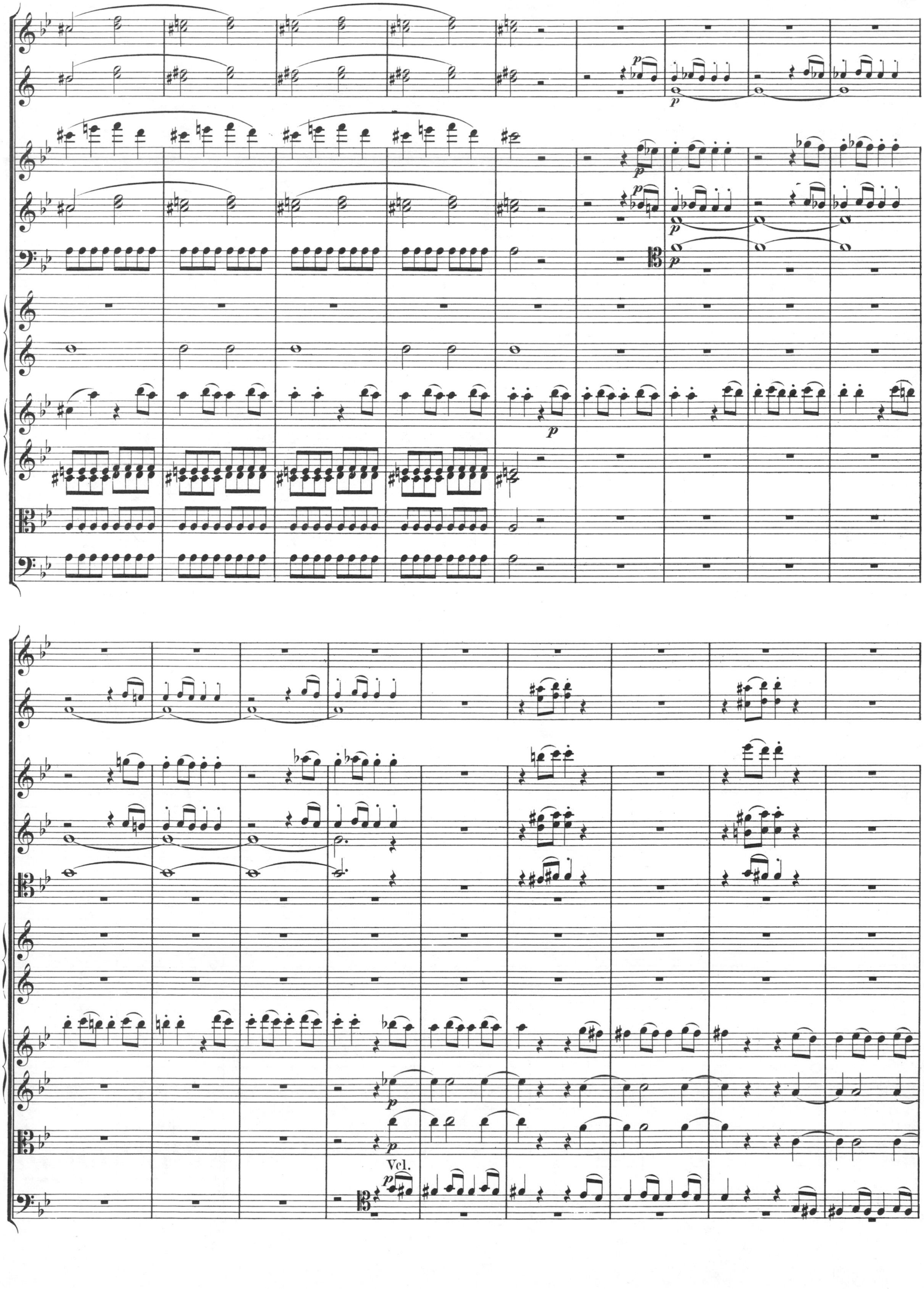
p
p
p
p
p
p
p
Vcl.
p

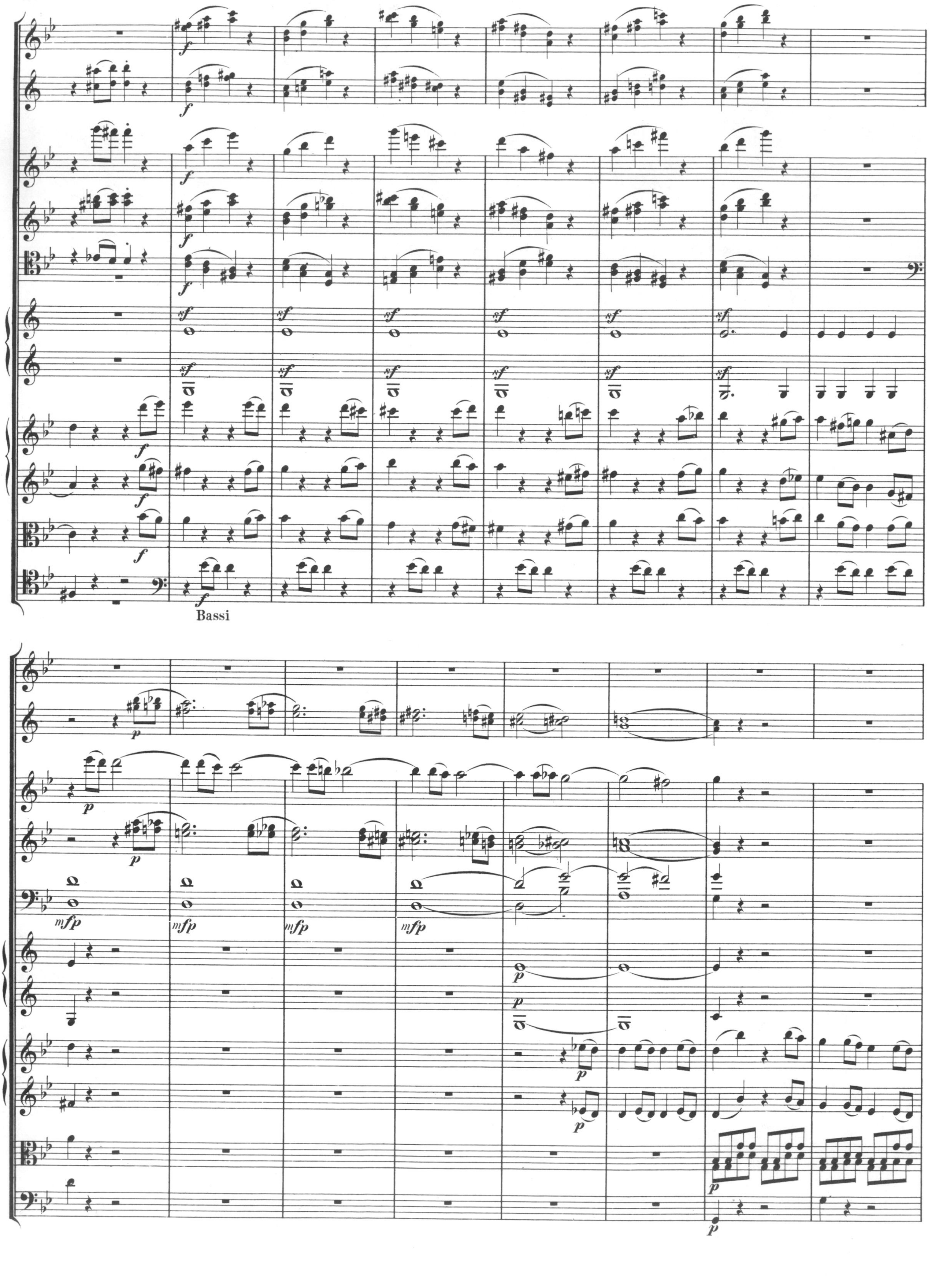
Bassi

198

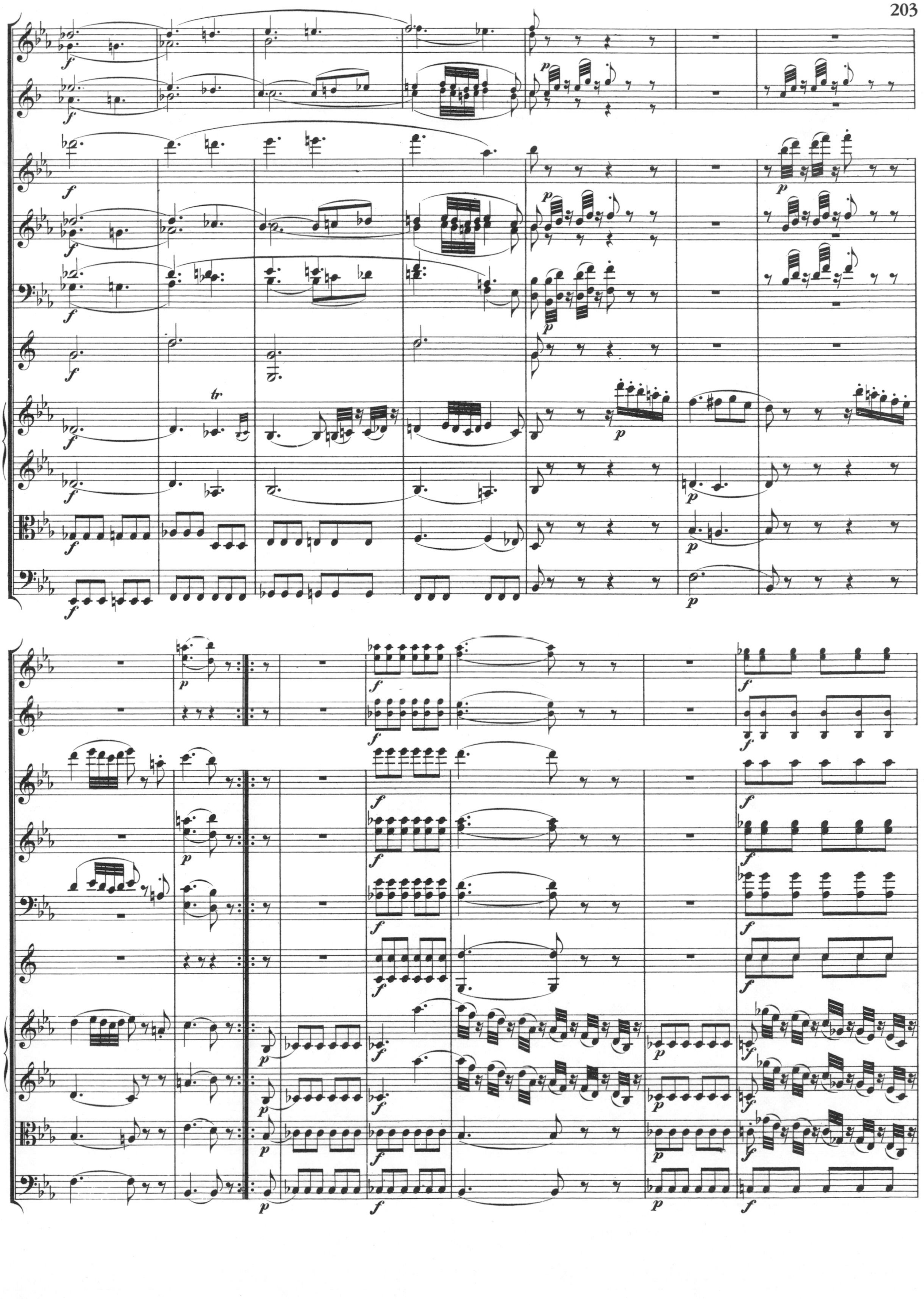

MENUETTO.
Allegretto.

Trio.

Menuetto da capo.

Allegro assai.

Oboi.

Clarinetti in B.

Flauto.

Oboi.

Fagotti.

Corno in B alto.

Corno in G.

Violino I.

Violino II.

Viola.

Violoncello
e Basso.

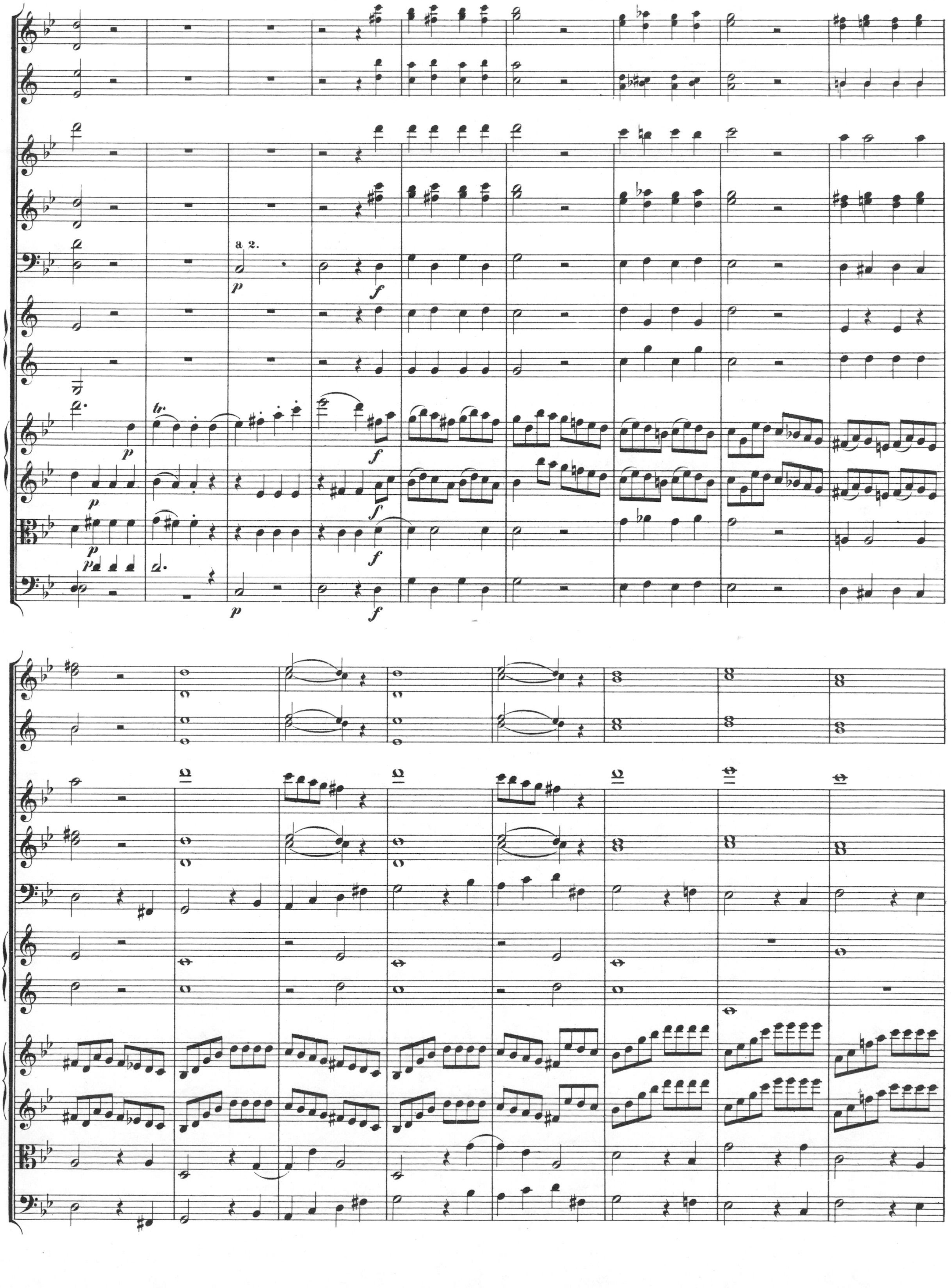
a 2.

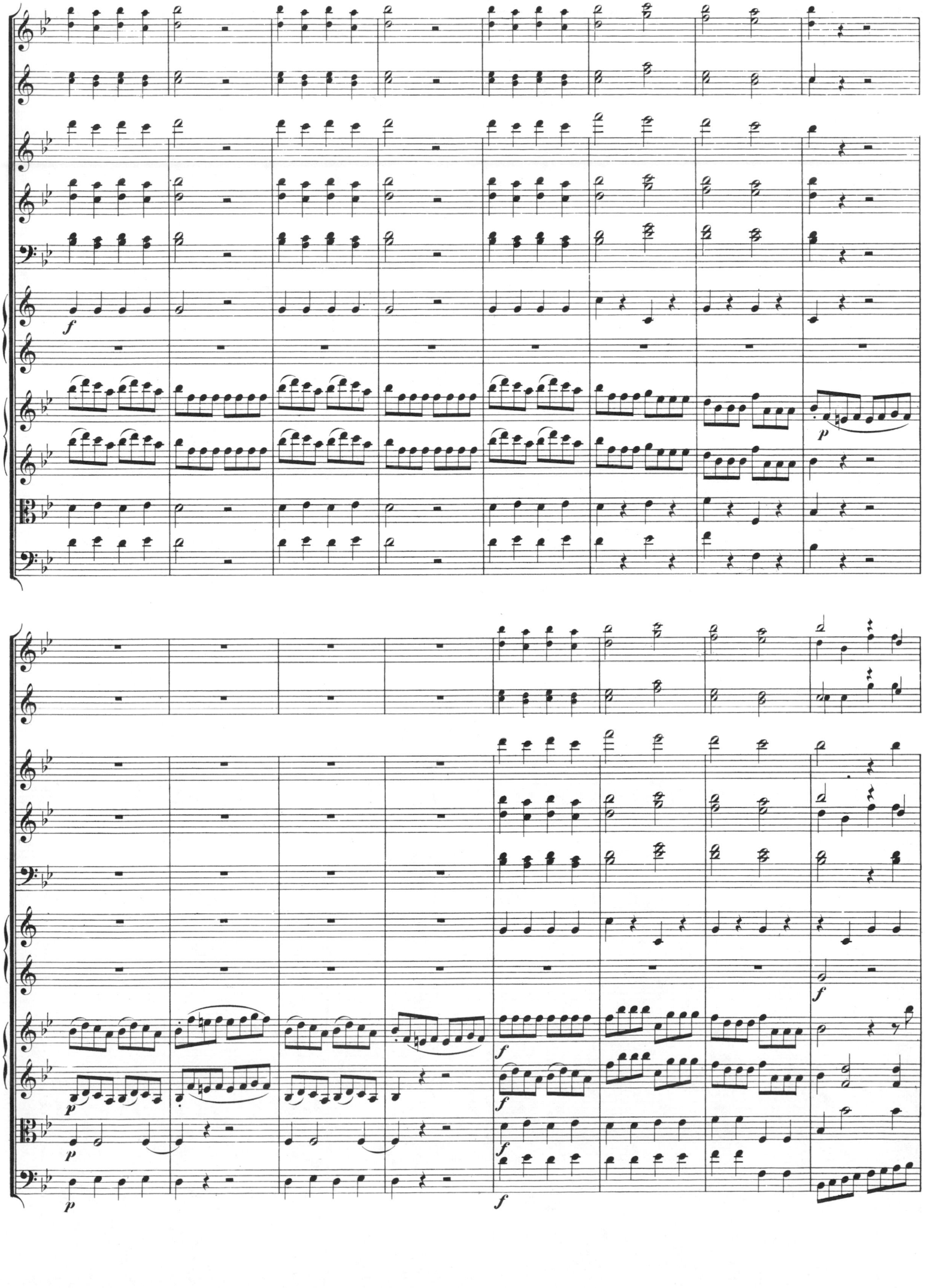
f
p
f
p
p
p
f
f
f
f
p

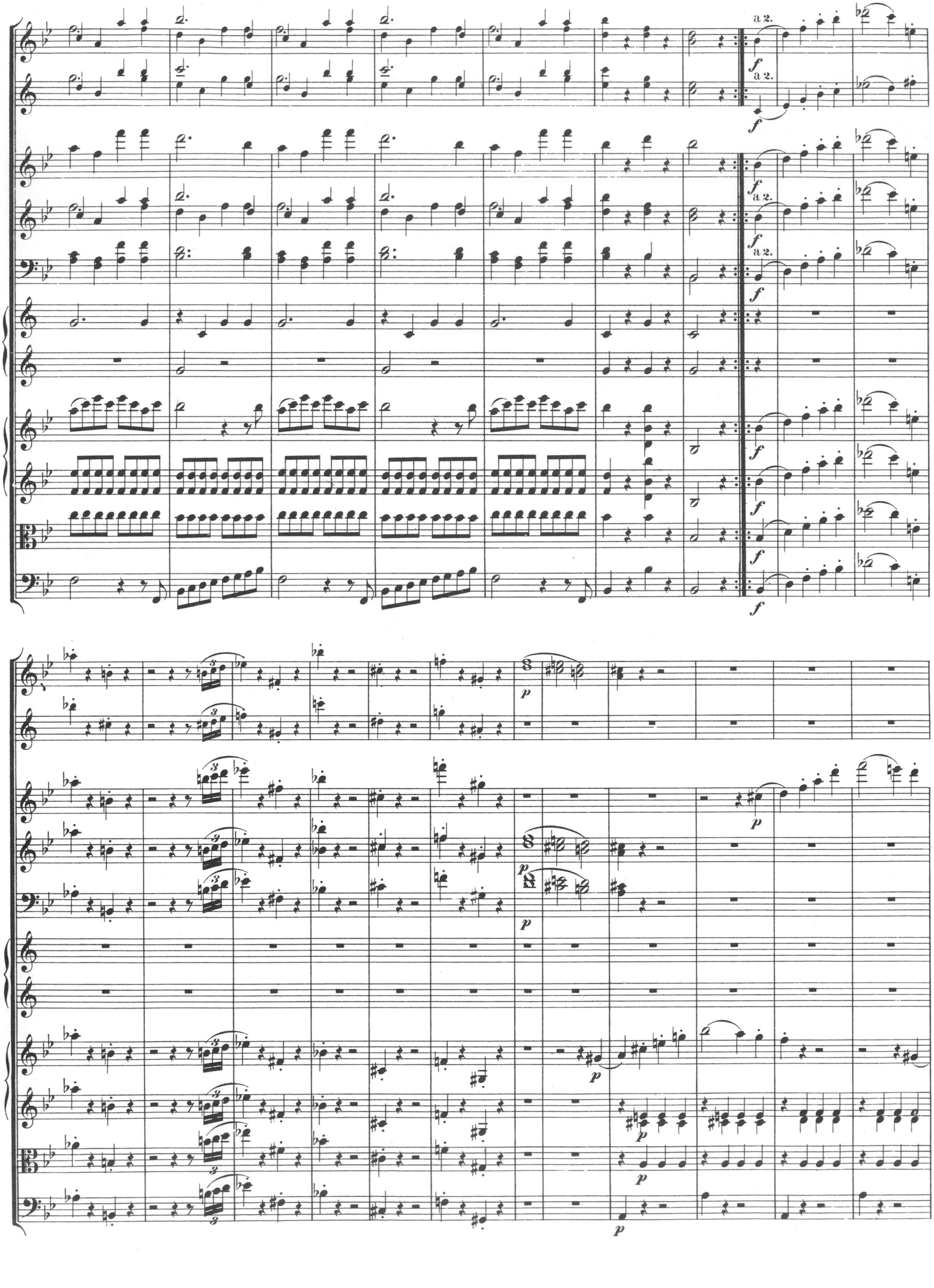
a 2.
f
a 2.
f
f
a 2.
f
a 2.
f
f
f
f
f
p
p
p
p
p
p
p
p

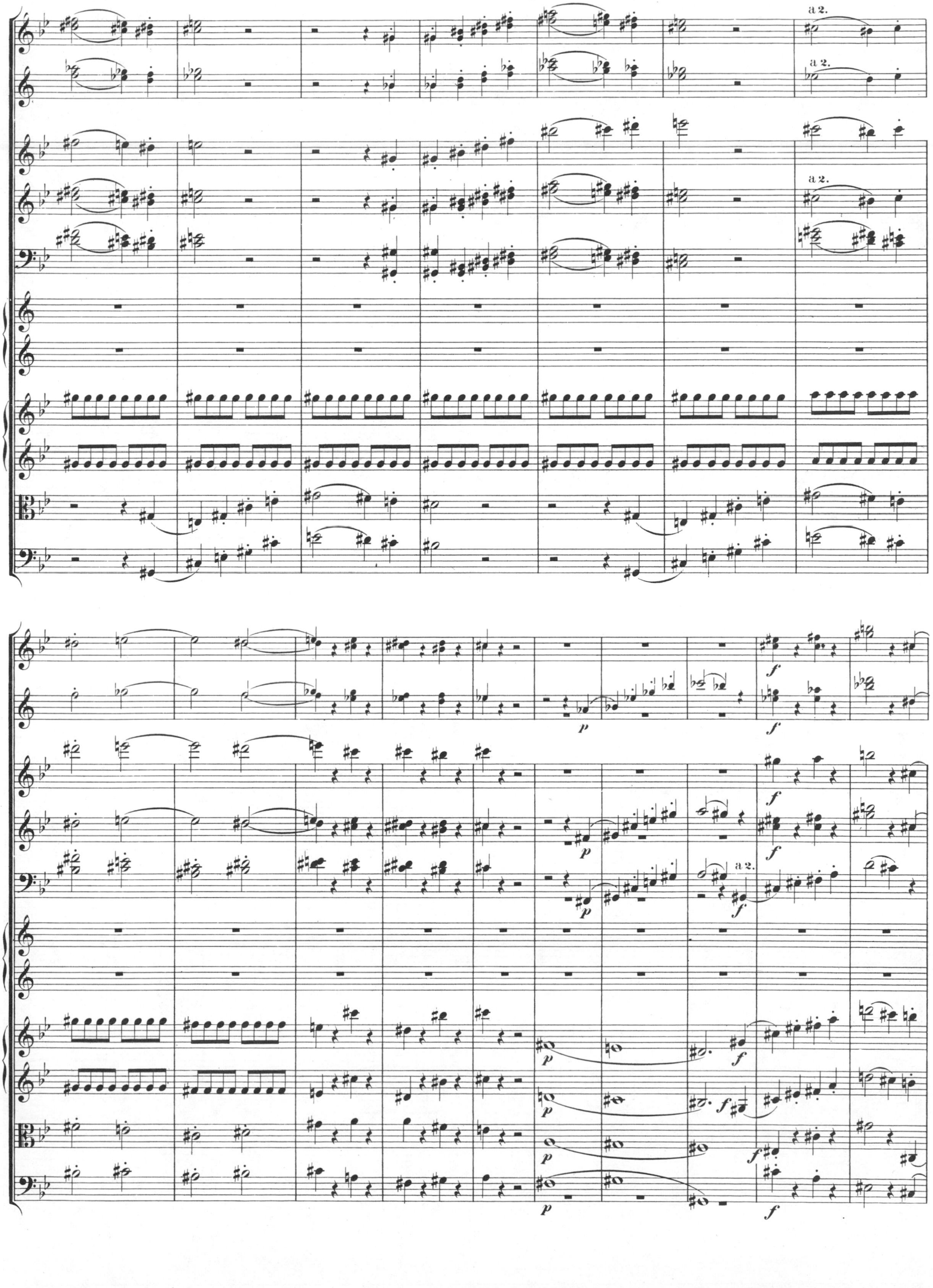
a 2.
a 2.
a 2.
a 2.

SYMPHONY No. 41

in C Major, K.551 ("Jupiter")

Completed August 10, 1788 in Vienna.

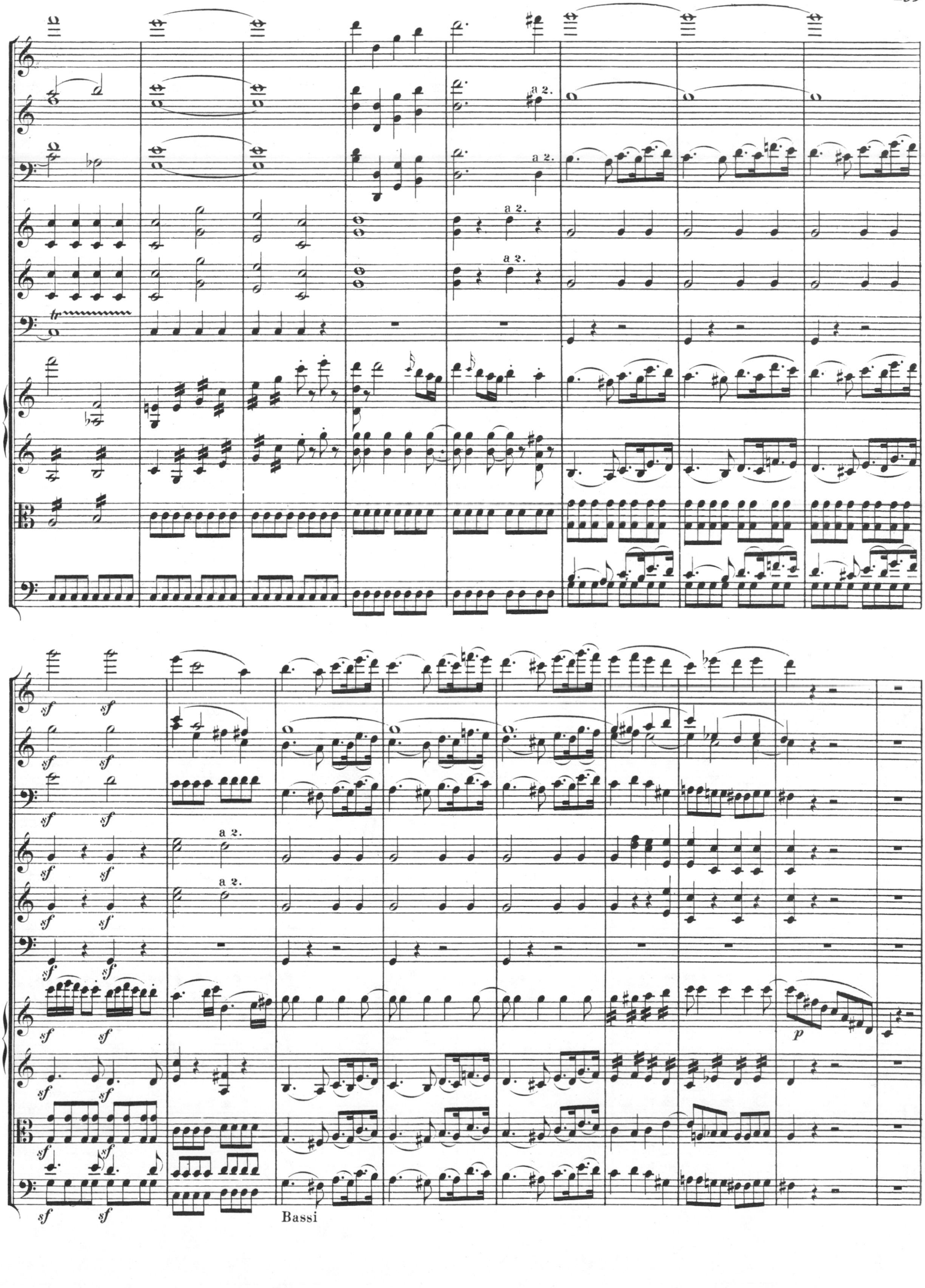
a 2.
a 2.
a 2.
a 2.
tr
sf
p
Bassi

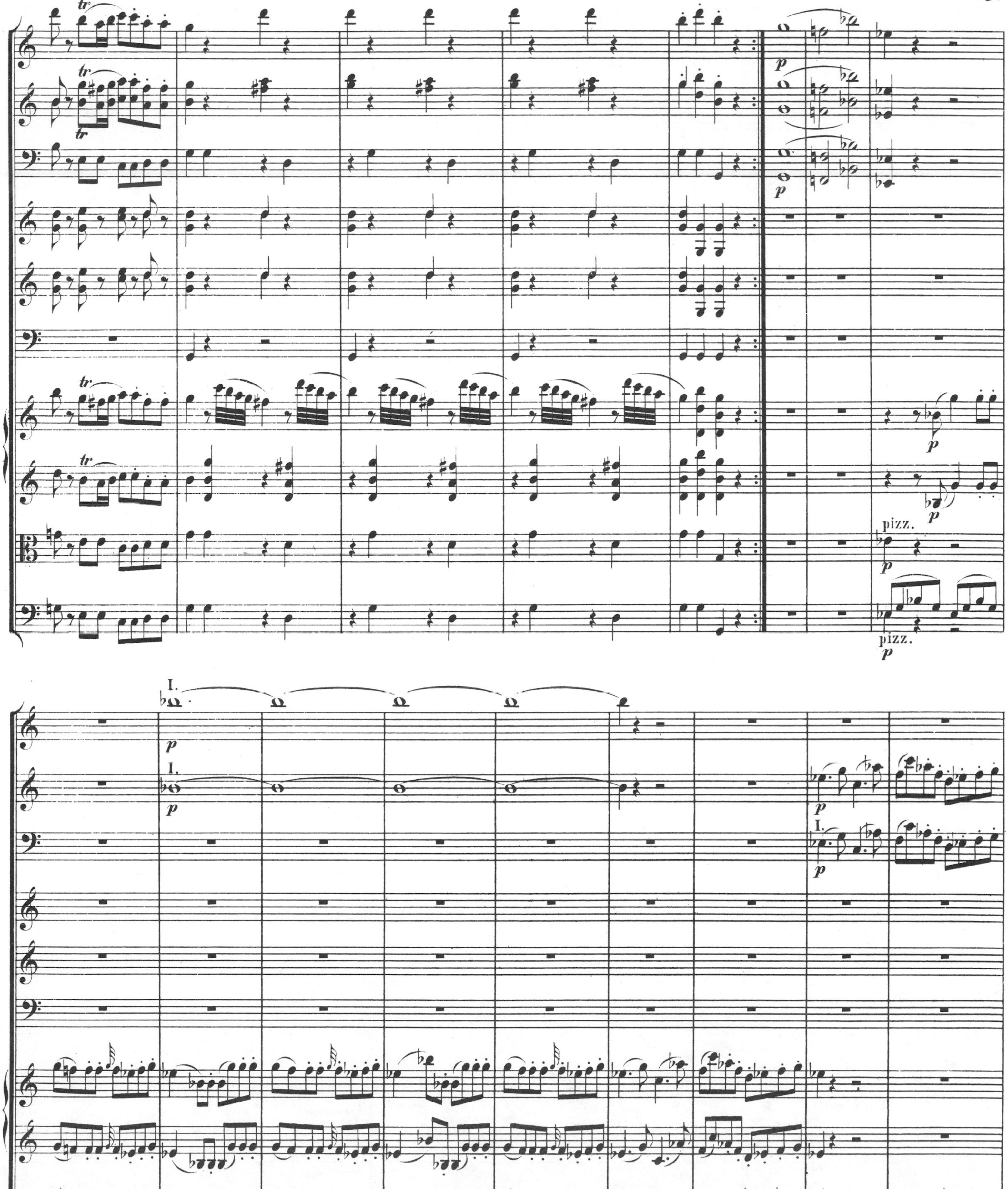
tr
p
I.
pizz.

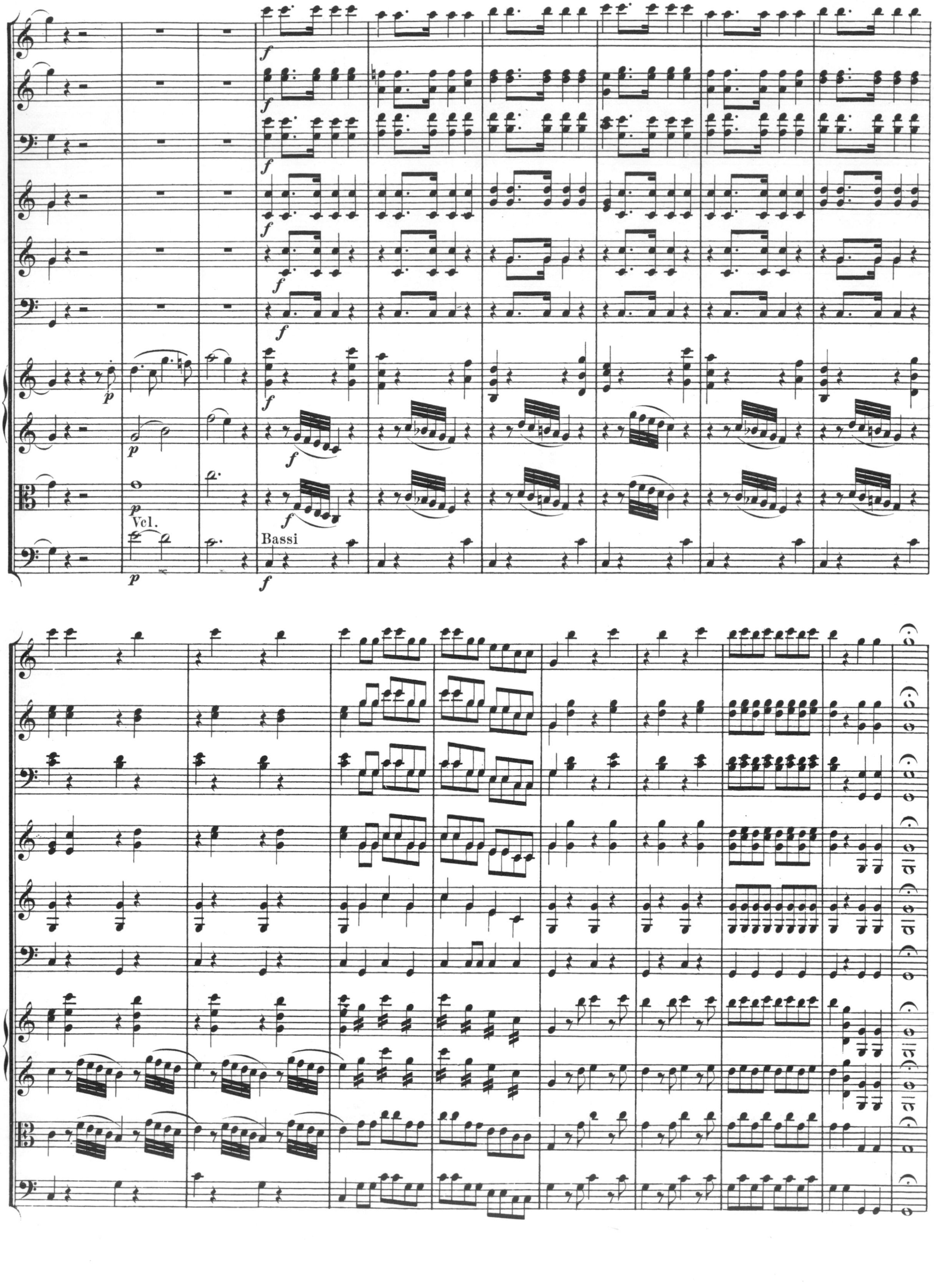
Vcl.
Bassi

Bassi

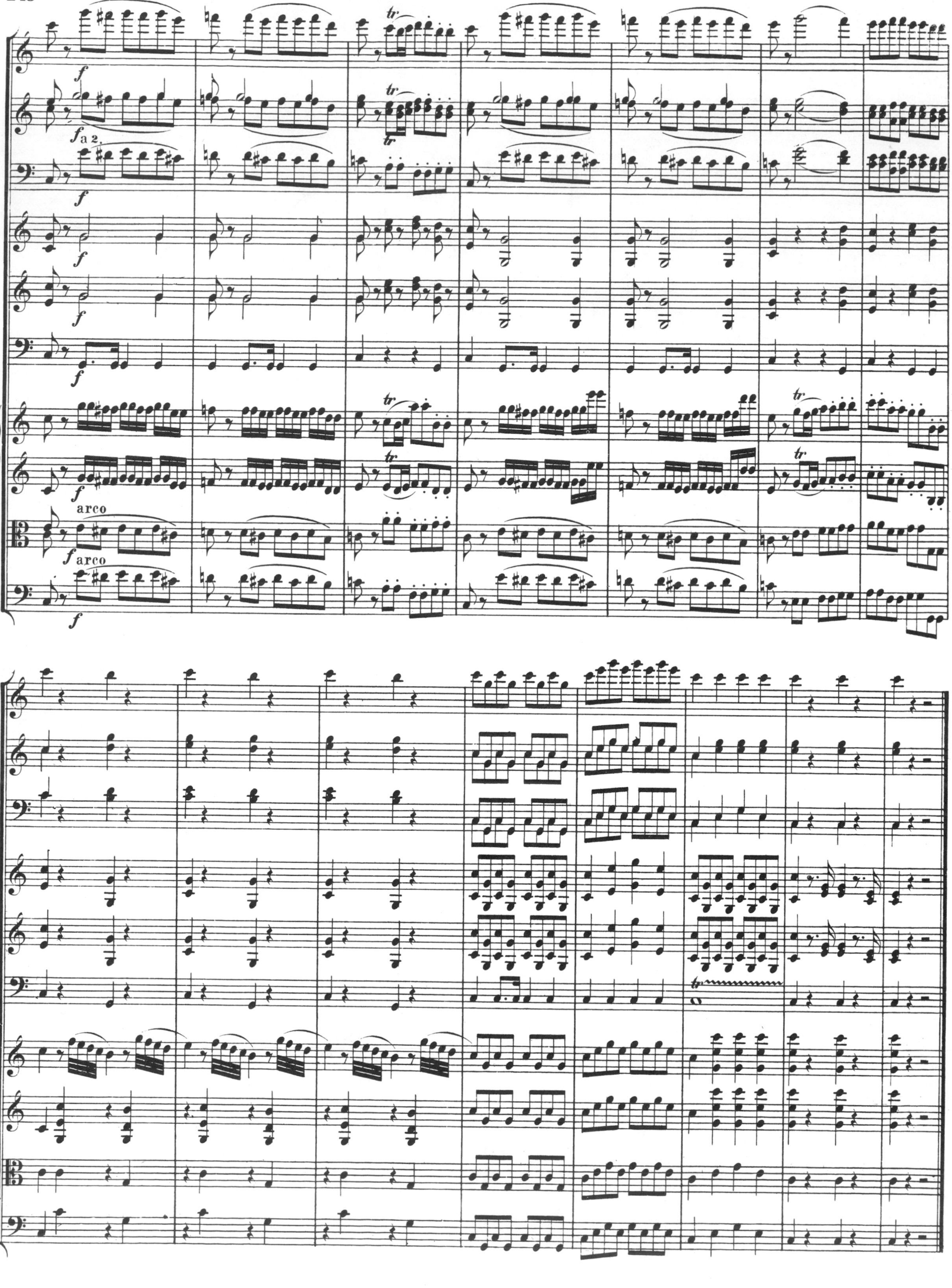
f
f a 2.
f
f
f
f
tr
tr
f
arco
f arco
f

Menuetto.

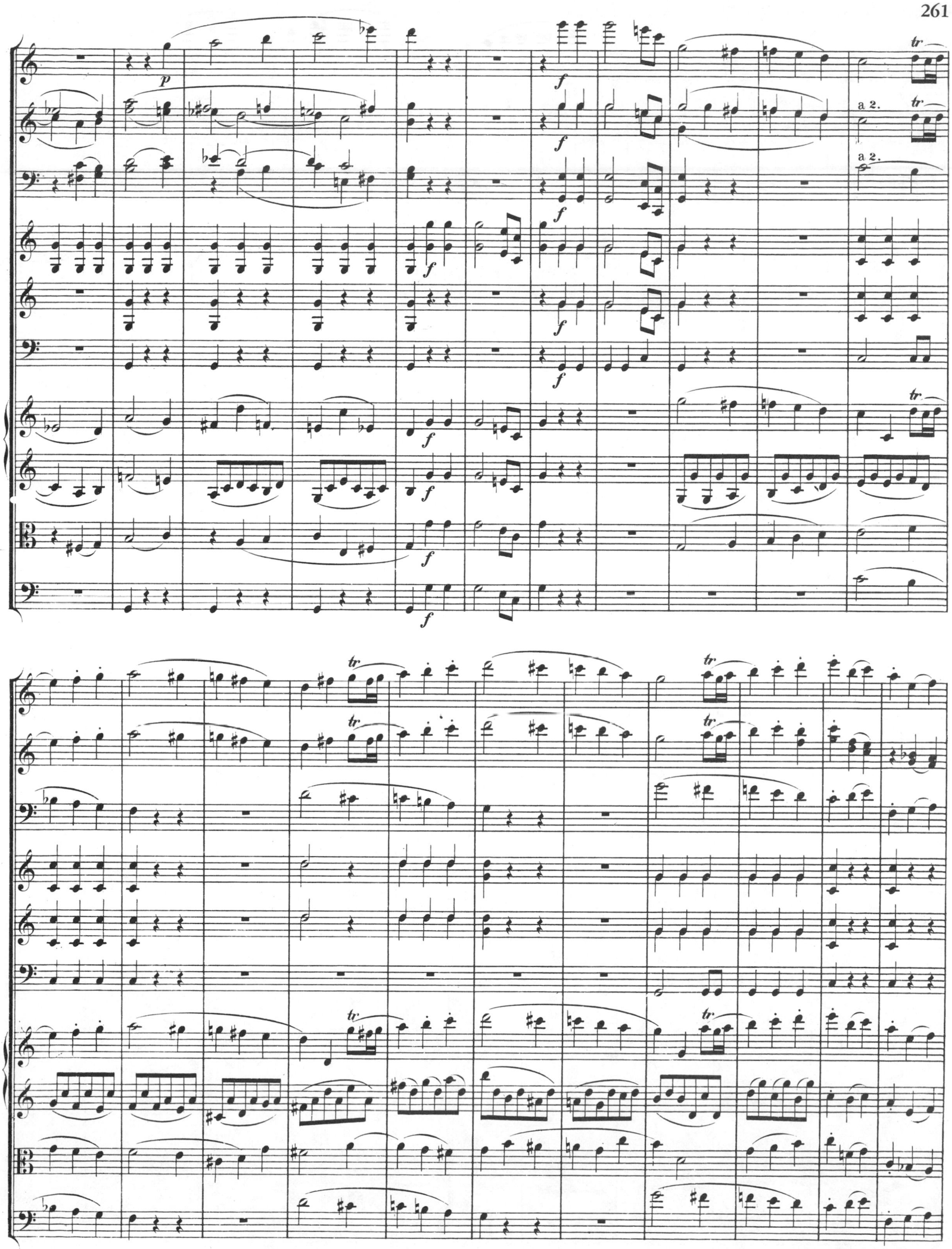
a 2.

TRIO.

Menuetto da capo

Molto Allegro.

Flauto.

Oboi.

Fagotti.

Corni in C.

Trombe in C.

Timpani in C.G.

Violino I.

Violino II.

Viola.

Violoncello
e Basso.

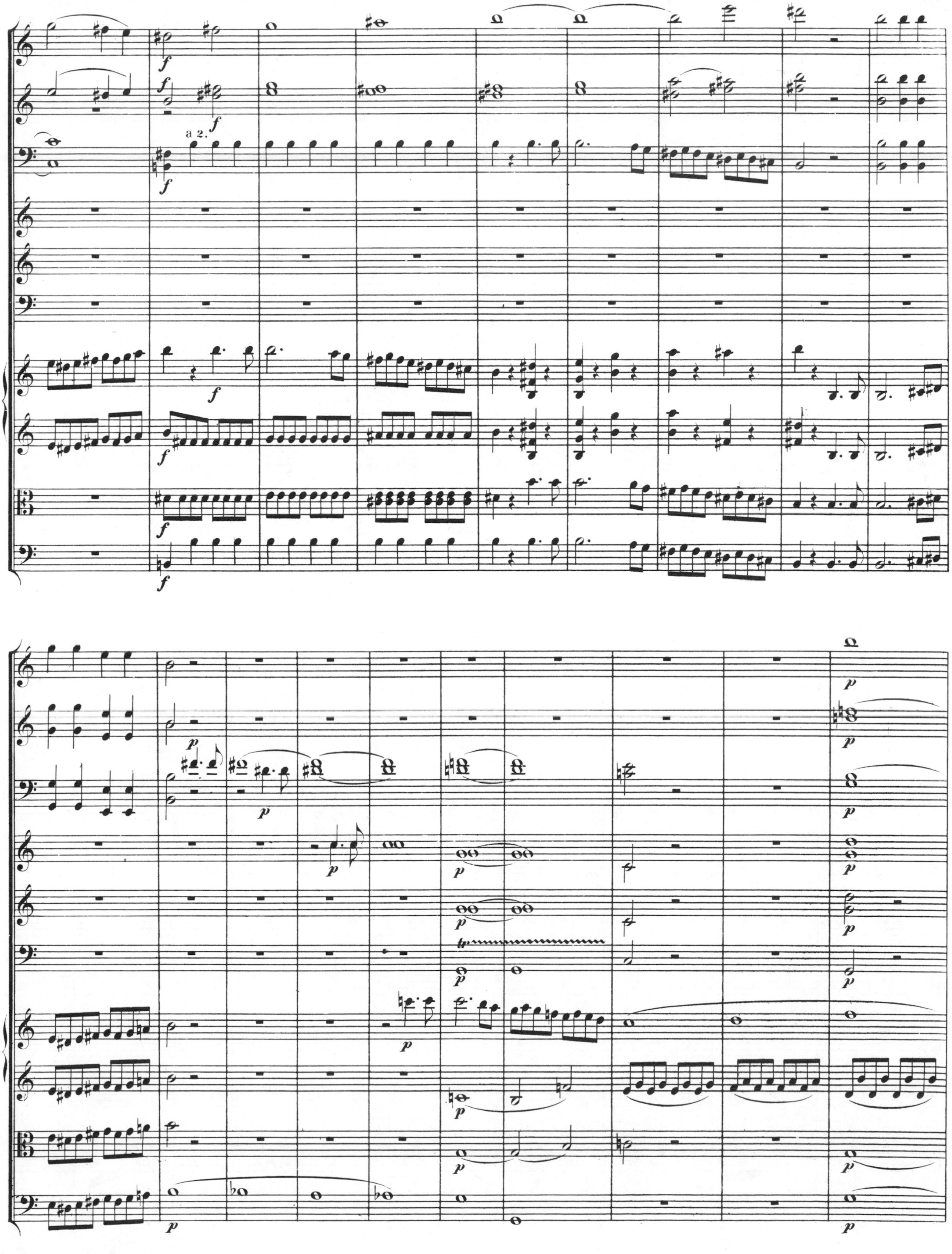
a 2.

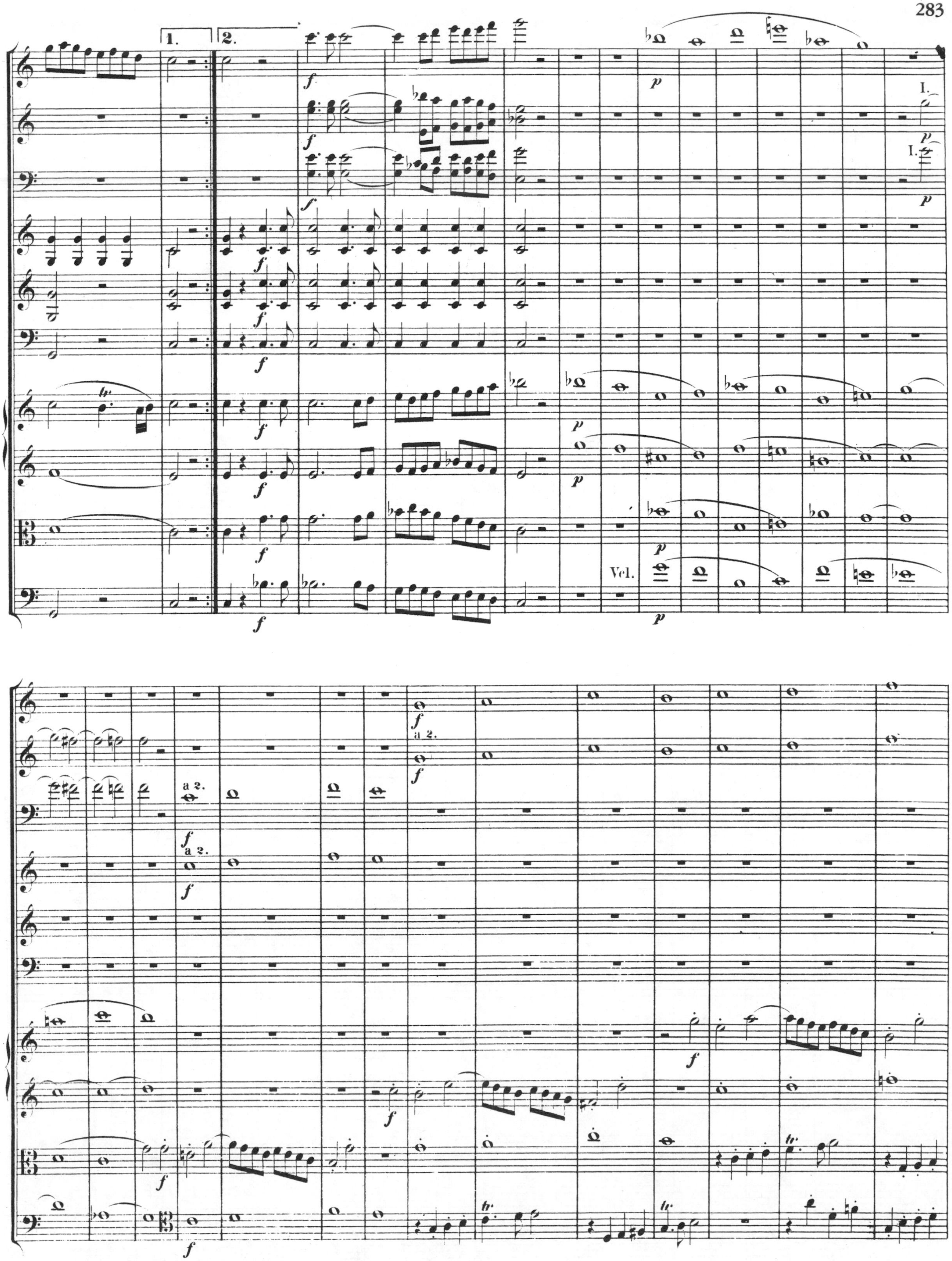
1.
2.
I.
a 2.
Vcl.

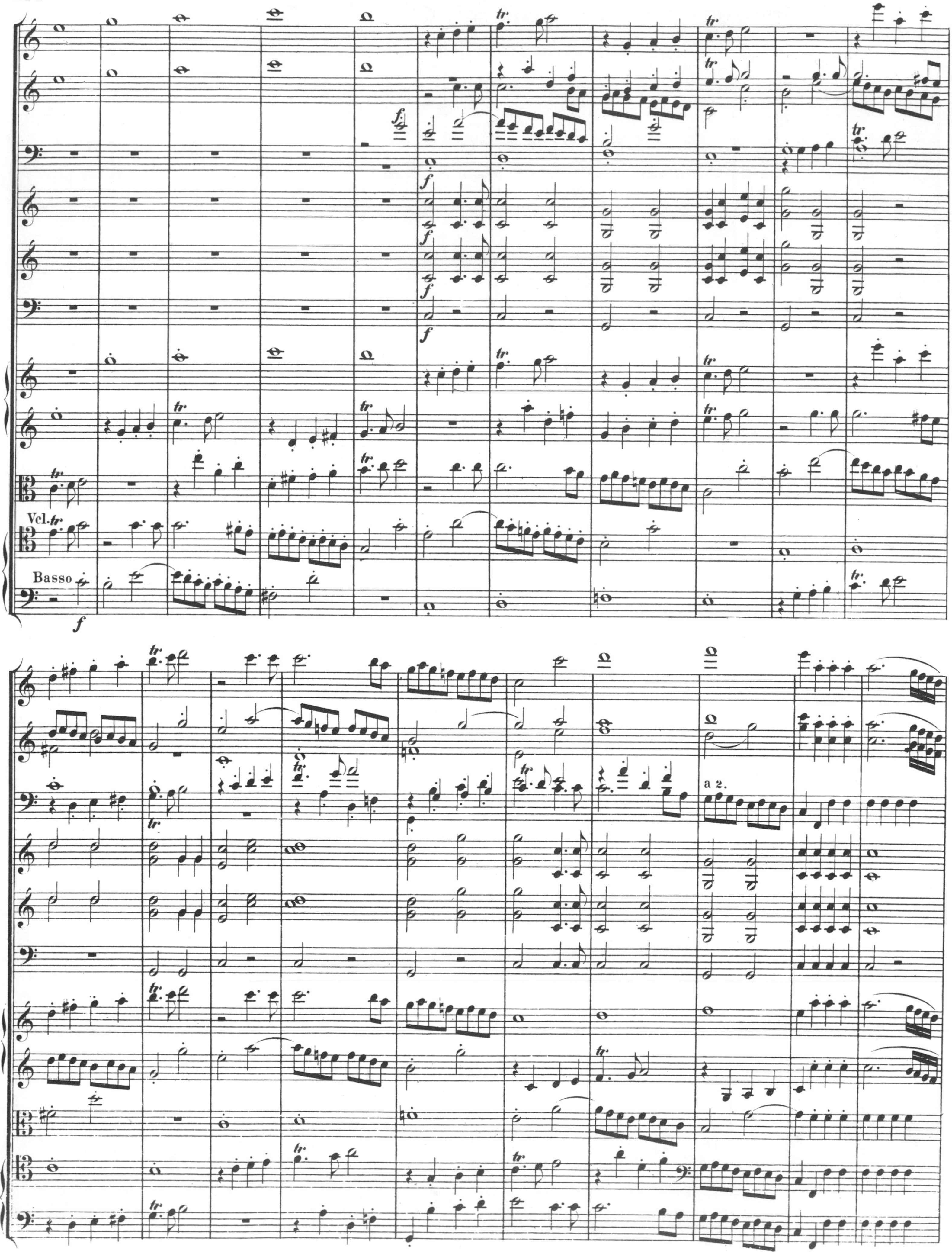
Vcl.
Basso
a 2.

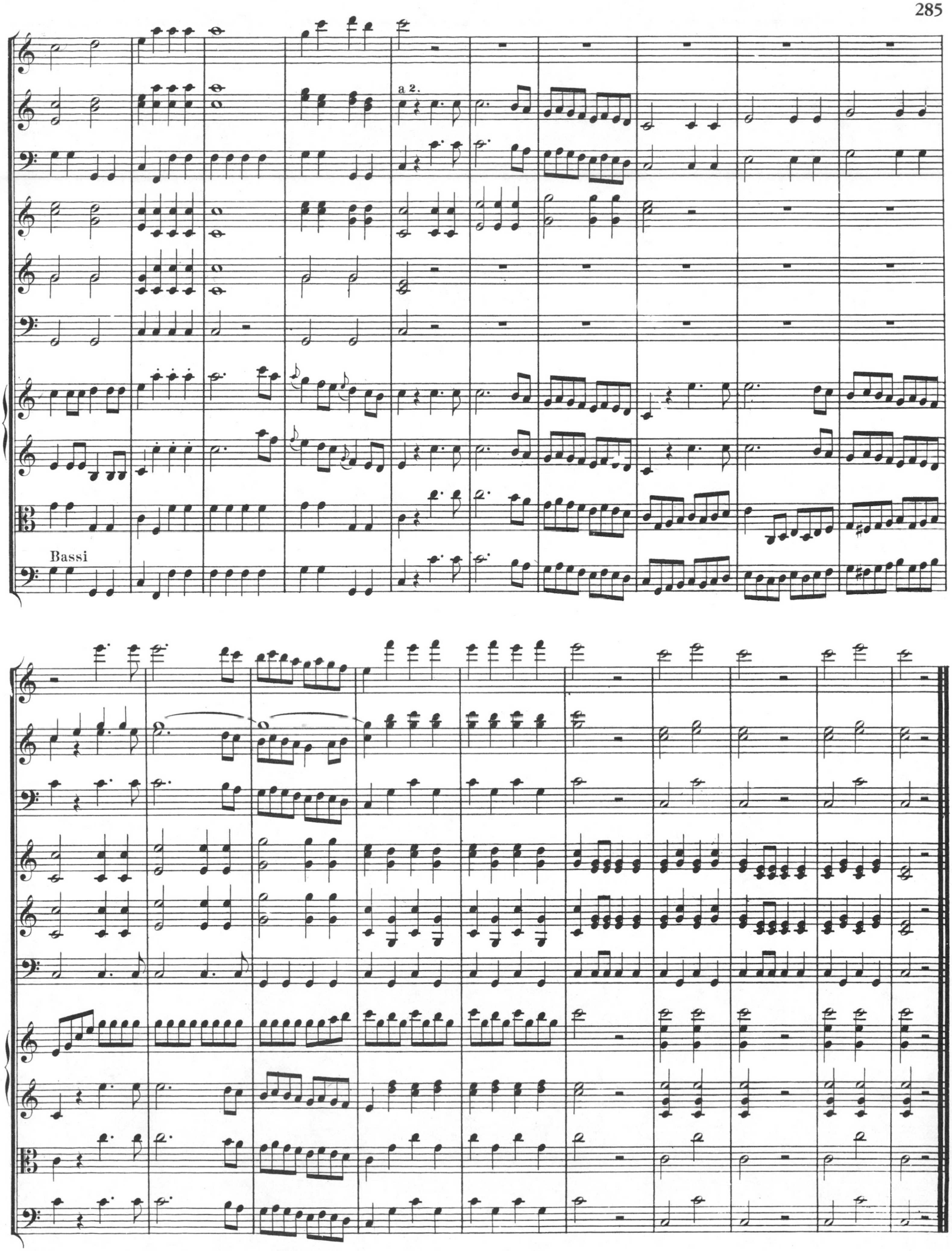
a 2.
Bassi